The Divine

Other Plays by
MICHEL MARC BOUCHARD

Christina, The Girl King (2014)*
The Coronation Voyage (1999)*
Desire: A Comedy (1997)
Down Dangerous Passes Road (2000)*
Heat Wave (1996)
Lilies, or, The Revival of a Romantic Drama (1997)
The Madonna Painter, or, The Birth of a Painting (2010)*
The Orphan Muses (1995)
The Tale of Teeka (1999)*
Tom at the Farm (2013)*
Written on Water (2004)*

* Published by Talonbooks

The Divine

A PLAY FOR SARAH BERNHARDT

Michel Marc Bouchard

Translated by Linda Gaboriau

TALONBOOKS

Talonbooks
278 East First Avenue, Vancouver, British Columbia, Canada v5T 1A6
www.talonbooks.com

First printing: 2015

Typeset in Arno
Printed and bound in Canada on 100% post-consumer recycled paper

Interior and cover design by Typesmith
Cover shows the painting *Portrait of Sarah Bernhardt* by Georges Clairin, 1876
Petit Palais, Paris

Talonbooks acknowledges the financial support of the Canada Council for the Arts, the Government of Canada through the Canada Book Fund, and the Province of British Columbia through the British Columbia Arts Council and the Book Publishing Tax Credit.

Library and Archives Canada Cataloguing in Publication

Bouchard, Michel Marc, 1958–
[Divine illusion. English]
    The divine : a play for Sarah Bernhardt / Michel Marc
Bouchard ; translated by Linda Gaboriau.

Translation of: La divine illusion : une pièce pour Sarah Bernhardt.
A play.
Issued in print and electronic formats.
ISBN 978-0-88922-958-7 (paperback).– ISBN 978-0-88922-959-4 (epub)

    1. Bernhardt, Sarah, 1844–1923 – Drama. I. Gaboriau, Linda, translator II. Title. III. Title: Divine illusion. English.

PS8553.O7745D5513 2015   C842'.54   C2015-904037-X
                                                   C2015-904038-8

For Jackie Maxwell
For Serge Denoncourt
Whose friendship, talent, and
respect nurture my work

What would life be without art?
Eating, drinking, sleeping, praying,
and dying ... Why go on living?

— SARAH BERNHARDT
Quebec City, December 1905

PREFACE

A blaze of light!

In December 1905 in Quebec City, Michaud, a young seminarian longing for the ecstasy of the theatre, dedicates his first play to his idol, The Divine Sarah Bernhardt, who – like a sudden blaze of light – has appeared in his sombre city.

The Divine is a fable about the meeting between this brilliant, mythical actress and this young man whose innocence is shattered by his growing awareness of the iniquities of his times.

The Divine is a play inspired by two shocking statements the famous actress made during her sojourn in Quebec City: one about the intellectual and artistic backwardness of our country and the other about the importance of art in society.

Today, lacking in culture and curiosity, most of our elite produce joylessness and bland comfort. Servants of anonymous shareholders, they sabotage hope. Anger and vulgarity dominate our culture as people become deaf to messages of change and idealism, and art gradually abandons the sublime for the acceptable.

Why revisit the past? Why evoke the memory of the contingents of young people conscripted by religious decrees? Why talk about children exploited in insalubrious factories? More than a century later, religious dogma continues to divide nations and motivate the murder of thousands of men, women, and children every day. Material greed shapes our lives more than ever, as it destroys our planet and enlists regiments of slave labour abroad for the fabrication of our countless household objects.

Are we entering a new dark age?

Sarah teaches Michaud that our ability to express our rebellion resides in the sources of light within us.

Despite my propensity to see everything that is wrong in this world, I still manage to see, every day, examples of social solidarity or human compassion, in reading a poem or listening to a song, in a dancer's gesture or the colour in a painting, in the tears of achievement or the excitement of a scientific discovery. Yes. I still manage to see blazes of light, and these moments of hope are divine and motivate me to carry on.

— MICHEL MARC BOUCHARD

PRODUCTION HISTORY

The Divine: A Play for Sarah Bernhardt was commissioned for the Shaw Festival and premiered at the Royal George Theatre in Niagara-on-the-Lake, Ontario, July 5 to October 11, 2015, playing in repertory with the following cast and crew:

MICHAUD: Ben Sanders
TALBOT: Wade Bogert-O'Brien
MRS. TALBOT: Mary Haney
LEO: Kyle Orzech
BROTHER CASGRAIN: Martin Happer
EMMA FRANCOEUR: Catherine McGregor
THÉRÈSE DESNOYERS: Jenny L. Wright
THE BOSS: Ric Reid
SARAH BERNHARDT: Fiona Reid
MEYER: Andrew Bunker
MADELEINE: Darcy Gerhart
JOURNALISTS:
Billy Lake
Catherine McGregor
Jonathan Tan
Jenny L. Wright

Directed and dramaturged by Jackie Maxwell
Designed by Michael Gianfrancesco
Lighting designed by Bonnie Beecher
Original music and sound designed by John Gzowski
Stage managed by Diane Konkin
Stage management assistance by Andrea Schurman

The Divine

A PLAY FOR SARAH BERNHARDT

CHARACTERS

MICHAUD
A young seminarian from a wealthy family

TALBOT
A young seminarian from a poor family

MRS. TALBOT
A widow, the mother of Talbot and Leo,
works in a shoe factory

LEO
Talbot's younger brother, works in a shoe factory

BROTHER CASGRAIN
A distinguished-looking man who personifies the
status of the Grand Seminary

EMMA FRANCOEUR and THÉRÈSE DESNOYERS
Workers in the shoe factory

THE BOSS
Factory owner

SARAH BERNHARDT
Illustrious French actress on tour in Quebec City

MEYER
Sarah Bernhardt's manager

MADELEINE
A young actress, member of Sarah Bernhardt's troupe

JOURNALISTS
(or JOURNALISTS' VOICES OFF)

SETTING

The action takes place in December 1905 in Quebec City.
The different places suggested (the stage, dressing room,
and artists' entrance of the theatre and the factory) are all
evoked in the dormitory of the prestigious Grand Seminary
(*Grand Séminaire de Québec*).

ACT ONE

THE DORMITORY

The dormitory at the Grand Seminary. Several cast-iron beds with chairs and nightstands. Two rows of high, mullioned windows. The overall effect is reminiscent of Jean-Paul Lemieux's paintings dominated by almost transparent tones of pearl white and pale grey.

MICHAUD, dressed in the seminarian's uniform of white shirt and dark pants, is holding binoculars and standing at the top of a ladder looking out an open window. It is snowing. He's trying to see something. Only the seminary bell tower is visible.

TALBOT enters, a bandage on his forehead and a bag slung over his shoulder, accompanied by MRS. TALBOT, his mother, who is carrying a small suitcase.

MRS. TALBOT
  What a great day, my boy. What a great day. Windows high as church steeples. And lily-white beds! This is no seminary, it's a palace. (*breathing in the smell of a pillowcase*) It smells of spring in the middle of December.

MICHAUD
  That's not the right bed. That's my bed. His is the one next to it. Put the pillow back! You have to shake it and slap it to give

it volume. Make sure the tips are straight. And you finish by smoothing the wrinkles with your hand. You can store his belongings in the bedside table. Little items in the top drawer, the bigger ones in the bottom. Never store food there. They can't stand the idea that we could eat anything but the cattle feed they serve us. If you run out of room, there's a locker in the hallway. You can take the one with no name on the door. (*by rote*) Up at five o'clock. Five minutes for ablutions. Morning mass then classes and study periods ... Welcome!

> *TALBOT takes off his winter coat. He is wearing street clothes. His mother lays out the meagre contents of the suitcase on her son's bed.*

MRS. TALBOT
Two white shirts, brand new, nice 'n starched.

MICHAUD
Two starched shirts.

MRS. TALBOT
One pair of grey wool trousers. One pair of grey cotton. Brand new.

MICHAUD
One pair of wool trousers. One cotton pair.

MRS. TALBOT
One black blazer.

MICHAUD
One blazer.

> *MRS. TALBOT and TALBOT stare at MICHAUD.*

MICHAUD
Costumes. Accessories. I like to take notes.

> *MRS. TALBOT sits down on the bed.*

MICHAUD
We're not allowed to sit on the beds.

TALBOT
(*firmly*) You can sit, Ma.

MICHAUD
We're not allowed –

TALBOT
You can sit.

MICHAUD
(*resigned*) Fine. I'll show you how to smooth the wrinkled sheets later.

MRS. TALBOT
Sometimes my leg goes all numb. It's 'cause of the damn pedal on the machine.

TALBOT
Take off your boots. Give me your feet.

MRS. TALBOT
Good Lord, it's Christmas three weeks ahead of time.

> *MRS. TALBOT takes off her boots. TALBOT massages her feet. Sound of a train whistle in the distance.*

MICHAUD
They mentioned a Pullman. In the newspaper, they said she has a parlour car all to herself. All silver from stem to stern. (*looking through a pair of binoculars*) I borrowed Brother Casgrain's binoculars. I told him I wanted to see the ice floes on the river. A lie! I'll confess it.

MRS. TALBOT
She's all the women at the factory can talk about. The tickets to that play of hers cost the price of an inheritance and I hear they're sold out! That actress's arrival's a big event.

MICHAUD
It's more than an event, it's a revolution! Quebec City will never be the same. Sarah chose our little city and our little city has stage

7

fright. Stage fright is the overwhelming feeling that takes hold of you before you go onstage.

MRS. TALBOT

They say she doesn't look her age. Easy not to look your age, with all them fancy Parisian creams she puts on her face. They're makin' them with veal marrow these days. You couldn't pay me to rub cow fat on my face, just to look younger. Over my dead body. I'd rather keep my old wrinkles than smear 'em with lard.

TALBOT

Give me your other foot.

MRS. TALBOT

And don't get me goin' 'bout her lipstick. It's made with whale lungs. Not for me, thanks, I'd rather keep my dry old lips than grease 'em with whale lungs. They say young men should stay away from her. She devours them with her eyes.

MICHAUD

I'll have my cassock to protect me.

MRS. TALBOT

A woman like her'll drool at the idea of undoin' all those buttons.

Sound of a train whistle and clanging bell.

MRS. TALBOT

You hear that? The Pullman! It's entering the station. I've never seen such a long parlour car. There are so many journalists! And all those banners. Those flashes of powder.

Sound of a distant fanfare.

MICHAUD

You hear that? If I were there on the platform, I'd shout along with everyone: Sarah! Sarah! Victor Hugo's muse! Dumas's leading lady! The queen in *Ruy Blas*. It's you, Sarah! Rostand's *Aiglon*. You! A light in this dark world, let your spirit shine on us! I'm sure she's about to appear. (*beat*) Have you ever crossed the ocean, Mrs. Talbot?

MRS. TALBOT

Every day, sir. It's called the Sea of Trials and Tribulations.

MICHAUD

Once, my father, the minister of finance … I'm Minister
Michaud's son … my father, the minister of finance, took my
mother and me to Paris. One afternoon, he said: "Go explore,
the City of Light is yours." I got all dressed up and I hailed
the handsomest carriage in sight. When we reached my
destination, I entered a big hall. Red carpet, red curtains, red
upholstery! And crystal glass … No! Shards of stars! Suddenly
the lights went down. There was a deep silence. And she
appeared. Right in front of me. (*moved*) The hall was full,
but she was there just for me. Slim as a twig. Her hair on fire.
I tried to look like a man, I was a child. I was silent, I wanted
to shout. My eyes wanted to grab everything, my hands were
full of tears. When Sarah performs, words take wing, emotions
take root. (*acting lines from* Adrienne Lecouvreur, *quite well,
he climbs down the ladder dramatically*) "Life! All my efforts,
all my prayers, in vain! I feel my strength and my life slipping
away. Don't leave me. Soon my eyes will no longer see you,
my hand will no longer hold yours tight. Speak to me! Speak
to me!" (*collapsing and then crawling on the floor*) "Farewell,
glorious triumphs, divine art. My heart will beat no more with
these ardent emotions … Nothing survives us … Nothing but
remembrance. Farewell, my friends. Farewell." (*playing dead;
then silence*) Did you enjoy it? Did I overdo it when I fell? And
what about the death?

MRS. TALBOT

I was almost afraid it was true.

MICHAUD

What was your favourite moment? If you didn't like it, I'll try to
understand. What was your favourite moment?

MRS. TALBOT

The death!

MICHAUD

I LOOOVE TO DIIIE! It's a fabulous play. She'll be performing it tomorrow night. It's the story of Adrienne Lecouvreur, a young actress who is abandoned by her older lover. At the end of the play, the Church excommunicates her, and she dies, poisoned.

MRS. TALBOT

(*sarcastically*) Good thing I can't afford a ticket, I would've known how it ends.

MICHAUD

(*taking a notebook out from under his mattress and reading a passage*) "When the lights go down and the audience falls silent, we all hold our breath. The curtain goes up and we discover the set. Who is going to enter through that door? Who will sleep in those beds? Who will climb that ladder? I love the theatre. I love the theatre because it isn't my life." (*closing his notebook*) Sarah has just arrived in our city, and I am stuck here.

TALBOT

Your train station stinks of coal and old engine oil. It reeks of rat shit and beggars' piss. Your Sarah feels sick to her stomach from the rocking of the train. She's cold. People are shouting her name in her face. Shoving her. She's white as a ghost. Your Sarah feels like throwing up!

MICHAUD

What's your name?

TALBOT

Talbot.

MICHAUD

Well, Talbot, you're wrong.

TALBOT

She hasn't come here for your revolution. She's come for our money.

MICHAUD

My name's Michaud, and I'm going to prove that you're wrong.

TALBOT

Actors wear funeral-home makeup. They fake their emotions. They cry through their mouths! They try to pass for rich in their cardboard sets. Aging actresses play young flirts. The oldest actor pretends to be the son of the youngest.

MICHAUD

You're wrong.

TALBOT

From fifty feet away, they say the nastiest things about the person sitting right beside them, and that person pretends not to hear them. They talk to themselves, question themselves, and answer themselves back! There are asylums for that kind of behaviour. Theatre's just a bunch of stories invented to make rich people cry. And you have to be rich to "looove to diiie."

MICHAUD

Where did you come from? How come you've shown up at the end of the semester? And what's your mother doing here? Don't you know that's forbidden? What did you do to deserve special treatment? And what about the bandage on your forehead? Were you in a fight? Over what? Why are you so bitter? That's what the audience has been wondering since you made your entrance.

LEO, Talbot's younger brother, enters.

LEO

I never seen so many doors.

MICHAUD

And who is he?

LEO

Leo.

MRS. TALBOT

His kid brother.

LEO
Hi.

MRS. TALBOT
You're late.

LEO
Easy to get lost in this place.

MICHAUD
You're not in school?

LEO
Who are you?

MRS. TALBOT
His name's Michaud.

MICHAUD
How old are you?

LEO
Twelve.

> MICHAUD *is taking notes.*

MRS. TALBOT
(*cutting him off*) You're late, you rascal.

LEO
(*to TALBOT*) Don't I look swell?

MRS. TALBOT
(*to MICHAUD*) A cousin lent him his suit.

LEO
(*proud*) Not every day ya get to visit your brother at the
Grand Seminary.

> LEO *goes to sit down.*

MRS. TALBOT
(*still sitting on the bed*) We're not allowed to sit on the beds.

LEO

Happy to see you again, Father!

TALBOT

I'm not a priest yet, Leo.

LEO

Listen to this one. There's this beggar who goes to stand before God.

MRS. TALBOT

(*to MICHAUD*) You'll get a kick outta this one.

LEO

He asks God: What's eternity like to you? God answers, for me, it's like one second. So, God, what's it like to have a million bucks? Well, to me, it's like one buck. Wow! So could you spare one buck for me? God answers, just wait one second.

Laughter.

MICHAUD

(*unenthusiastically*) Very funny.

MRS. TALBOT

(*to LEO*) You didn't wash before you put that suit on?

LEO

Didn't have time.

MRS. TALBOT

And you wiped yer nose on yer sleeve!

LEO

Didn't have a hanky.

MRS. TALBOT

Damn nosebleeds! If this keeps up, you'll have us payin' for a doctor. What a pair you two make. One's got a bloody nose, the other a banged-up forehead. Good thing I got four more at home who ain't such a mess. Come here.

> MRS. TALBOT *finds a handkerchief in her handbag*
> *and wipes Leo's nose.*

LEO

I hate it when you wipe my nose.

MRS. TALBOT

He's been gettin' these nosebleeds ever since they changed the glue at the shop.

LEO

It's not the glue. It's that new red.

MRS. TALBOT

Last week, the little Paquette girl had the same thing, before the machine cut her head off.

MICHAUD

Her head?!

MRS. TALBOT

When her little sister went to help 'er, the belt on the tanner grabbed her too. By the hair, like her sister.

MICHAUD

By the hair?

LEO

Didn't even have time to scream.

MRS. TALBOT

Thirteen and eleven years old.

MICHAUD

(*writing in his notebook*) Thirteen and eleven years old.

MRS. TALBOT

Gotta wear kerchiefs.

LEO

Because of them, they raided the shop yesterday. When the inspectors left, the women forgot to knock three times on the trap door so the kids would come out. We spent five hours in that stinkin' hole, breathin' in the red dye. (*stamping his foot three times*) Three knocks on the floor. Not that hard to remember. (*proudly, to his brother*) Hey, the boss promised me a puff on his cigar.

TALBOT
Lucky you!

> *LEO takes some money out of his pocket and hands it to TALBOT.*

LEO
Here, this is for you. For your new cassock.

TALBOT
(*upset*) Sweet Jesus. This is a fortune. It could buy me a cassock made of gold. (*giving his brother a hug*) My deepest gratitude, Leo.

LEO
"Gratitude?"

TALBOT
That means "thank you." Thank you, Leo.

LEO
I love it when you talk all proper. You hear that, Ma? "Gratitude."

> *MRS. TALBOT takes a pair of men's shoes, wrapped in a rag, out of her bag and hands them to TALBOT.*

MRS. TALBOT
These are for you too.

TALBOT
They're beautiful.

LEO
(*wiping his nose on his sleeve*) It's me who glued the soles. Look inside! Go ahead, look!

TALBOT

(*finding money in one of the shoes*) I don't know what to say, Ma.

LEO

"Gratitude?" Tell her, "gratitude."

TALBOT

(*smiling*) Gratitude, Ma.

> *MRS. TALBOT takes her son's hands and strokes them.*

MRS. TALBOT

(*to MICHAUD*) No kid in our family ever had such clean soft hands. So pink and pretty. Lifelines drawn so clear. I dunno how to read 'em but I'm sure they spell out a beautiful future. What a great day!

TALBOT

I have something for you too.

> *TALBOT takes several pieces of real silverware, wrapped in a cloth, out of his bag. MRS. TALBOT and LEO don't know what to make of this treasure.*

MRS. TALBOT

Sweet Jesus! What's that?

TALBOT

A present.

> *Beat.*

LEO

(*disapprovingly*) What d'ya mean a present?

MRS. TALBOT

(*nervous*) Where'd you get that?

TALBOT

Don't you like it?

MRS. TALBOT

It's just that –

LEO

She asked you where you got it.

TALBOT

It doesn't matter where I got it.

LEO

What d'ya mean, it doesn't matter?

TALBOT

It doesn't matter!

LEO

Those come from your other school?

TALBOT

They gave them to me.

LEO

You gotta be kidding. That would cost more than a year of my pay.

TALBOT

They gave them to me!

LEO

It's gonna cost us an arm and a leg to keep you here, and you
'spect us to believe they give you fancy silverware as a bonus?

TALBOT

They gave them to me!

LEO

A priest don't lie.

TALBOT

(*annoyed*) Are you happy, Ma?

LEO

A priest don't steal.

TALBOT

Are you happy?

LEO

And a priest don't get into fights.

MICHAUD

You got into a fight?

TALBOT

(*ripping the bandage off his forehead*) We were playing hockey.

LEO

But he was a priest!

MICHAUD

You got into a fight with a priest? Wow!

TALBOT

What's your problem, Leo? I got transferred here. The best place in town. And I just gave our mother the nicest present she'll ever get. What's your problem?

LEO

Do I hafta remind you why I'm bustin' my ass for twenty cents a day in a factory that stinks to high heaven? You know what I think about while I spread the goddamn glue on the soles of shoes all day long?

TALBOT

No swearing!

LEO

Glue the soles, glue the soles, glue, glue, and more friggin' glue ... You know what my poisoned brain is thinkin' 'bout? I'm thinkin' 'bout the day when I'm gonna be proud of my big brother in his new cassock, lyin' there, face down, about to vow that he will devote his life, body 'n soul, to the Good Lord. I think about the day people will stop lookin' at our mother like she's a beggar, and they'll see her as a pious woman who gave her son to the Church. And I think about me, and how they'll give me a better job because my brother's a priest.

TALBOT

Lower your voice!

LEO

Yesterday I spent five hours hidin' in a goddamn rat hole that
stinks of red, just because some people think I'm too young
to be workin'!

TALBOT

Don't swear!

LEO

All that for you! And for us! To make our shitty lives better.
If you get thrown outta here, after everything we done for
you, you won't be my brother anymore. You hear me? And
she won't be your mother.

MRS. TALBOT

Leo!

LEO

Tell him, Ma.

MRS. TALBOT

I can't say that.

LEO

TELL HIM!

MRS. TALBOT

I'll never say that.

LEO

Figure out a way to take that stuff back where it came from.
I'm goin' outside to smoke. I'll be waitin' for you, Ma.

LEO exits. MRS. TALBOT puts the silverware in her bag.

TALBOT

You should leave too, Ma.

MRS. TALBOT

Don't listen to him. It's a beautiful present.

TALBOT

You can leave now.

MRS. TALBOT

Take care of them cuts.

TALBOT

Leave, Ma! For God's sake!

MRS. TALBOT

I'm leaving my boy with you, Mr. Michaud.

MRS. TALBOT exits. Silence.

MICHAUD

Did you steal it all at once, or piece by piece? Were you afraid
of getting caught? They say the fear of getting caught is like
a drug. They say your breathing gets constricted, your palms
get clammy, your heart beats faster. You have to tell me all
about the silverware. And you have to tell me about your fight
too. Is it true that we lose our minds when we start to punch?
That we get carried away and almost go mad? And the more we
punch, the harder it is to stop? Bang, bang, bang! (*beat*) You're
under my supervision, you have to tell me everything. You're
my first real thief. The others were only in books. Everyone
around here tells such boring stories. We're just spoiled rich
kids who make these tragic faces over nothing. We were caught
cheating. We're missing a pebble in our stone collection. Who
cares? With you, there are real fights and children who die
in factories. YOU are just what I needed. Dark, mysterious.
An authentic character, at last! I'm really happy you're here.

*MICHAUD gives TALBOT a pat on the back, but TALBOT
shoves him roughly and MICHAUD falls down.
TALBOT jumps on him and threatens him with his fist.*

TALBOT

(*trying to contain his rage*) You want to know what happens when
you start to punch someone? You really want to know? You want
to know how it feels when you can't stop? You really want to
know? You want me to fix your face like we fix a pillow that's been
messed up? You want me to slap your face to give it some volume?

MICHAUD

Let go of me!

TALBOT

You touch me again ... you hear me?

MICHAUD

All right!

TALBOT

Just once ...

MICHAUD

All right!

TALBOT

You put your paws on me again, just once, and I'll smash your
skull like a steer on slaughter day. You hear me?

> *MICHAUD manages to break away from TALBOT.*

MICHAUD

(*trying to regain his composure*) "Blessed are the peacemakers,
for they shall be called the children of God." Saint Matthew,
chapter 5, verse 9.

> *Beat.*

TALBOT

(*calmer*) You asked for it.

MICHAUD

"Recompense to no man evil for evil."

TALBOT

You shouldn't have touched me.

MICHAUD

"Provide things honest in the sight of all men. And live peaceably with all men." Letter to the Romans.

TALBOT

Chapter 12.

> Brother CASGRAIN enters, holding two cassocks and two white lace surplices. He stands in the background.

MICHAUD

(*recovering from what just happened*) Wow! That was ... that was great.

TALBOT

My family's workin' themselves to the bone so I can become a priest. A priest! Not a doctor or a lawyer. A priest! The only job possible for a poor kid who wants to escape poverty.

CASGRAIN

(*stepping out of the shadows*) Mr. Michaud!

MICHAUD

(*hiding his notebook under his mattress*) Brother Casgrain!

CASGRAIN

How are the ice floes on the river doing? Are they as active as the crowds rushing to greet the famous actress? (*firmly*) Give me my binoculars! I took a vow of obedience, not a vow of idiocy. Close that window. It's freezing in here.

> MICHAUD goes to close the window and the shutters.

CASGRAIN

You could have fallen out the window, a shortcut to eternity. Give me my binoculars! (*to TALBOT*) Welcome, Mr. Talbot. I'm Brother Casgrain, I see that you've met Mr. Michaud?

TALBOT

We're already friends.

CASGRAIN

He will familiarize you with life in our institution. Some
influential people believe that Mr. Michaud's "lively yet serene
mind," which I personally would call turbulent and exalted, will
be beneficial to your soul at this point. (*solemnly, indicating the
cassocks and surplices*) His Excellency, the archbishop, has chosen
the two of you to serve at morning mass.

MICHAUD

Why him?

CASGRAIN

Some of us, including my humble self, will never have this honour.
Do I feel envy? Certainly. I'll confess it. Do I enjoy expressing this
envy? Certainly. I'll confess that as well.

MICHAUD

(*enthusiastically, to TALBOT*) For the archbishop's vesting, you
begin with the alb. Followed by the dalmatic and the pallium.
Then the cincture and the gold girdle … the stole, the maniple,
the splendid chasuble, the pectoral cross. And you finish
with the cope.

CASGRAIN

There are no ceremonial vestments for morning mass.

MICHAUD

That's what I was about to say.

CASGRAIN

Mr. Michaud?

MICHAUD

Yes, Brother?

CASGRAIN

Did you really see that actress step down from her railway car?

MICHAUD
Her Pullman, Brother! It's called a Pullman!

CASGRAIN
Can you describe her arrival in detail?

MICHAUD
She had a friendly smile and a warm word for everyone.

CASGRAIN
And the expressions on her face?

MICHAUD
I can imitate every one of them.

CASGRAIN
I know you love theatre because it isn't your life.

MICHAUD
(*stunned*) You read my preface?

CASGRAIN
Our lives might not be as magical as you would like –

MICHAUD
You read my notebook!

CASGRAIN
… but they can become hell on earth if we ignore reality. You saw nothing of that woman's arrival.

MICHAUD
I can describe her better than all the people who were there to greet her.

CASGRAIN
There's a steeple that obstructs the view of the train station from that window. You saw nothing. Give me my binoculars.

MICHAUD hands him the binoculars.

MICHAUD
I would give anything to see her again.

CASGRAIN
I took the liberty of telling the archbishop about your passion for the theatre.

MICHAUD
The archbishop?

CASGRAIN
I told him about your talent for impersonations ... And your overactive imagination ...

MICHAUD
Really ... ?

CASGRAIN
And your tendency to dramatize everything ...

MICHAUD
And ... ?

CASGRAIN
After the mass, you will be going to the Atelier Theatre.

MICHAUD
(*incredulous*) What?

CASGRAIN
You're going to meet her!

MICHAUD
Meet who?

CASGRAIN
Sarah Bernhardt.

MICHAUD
I'm going to see her again! I'm going to ... Me? (*reciting a speech from* Adrienne Lecouvreur) "How delightful. I'm going mad. I laugh. I cry. I am dying of pain and of joy!"

CASGRAIN
(*handing him a letter*) You will deliver this letter to her in person.

MICHAUD

A letter?

CASGRAIN

You will read it aloud to her.

MICHAUD

Oh … I'll give my best performance.

CASGRAIN

It's a notice from His Excellency forbidding her to appear onstage in our city.

MICHAUD

(*stunned*) Me … Forbidding The Divine to perform?

CASGRAIN

How dare you take our Creator's name in vain? How dare you apply His supreme attribute to that woman! "The great priestess of immodesty" would be a more fitting name.

MICHAUD

A bit long for introductions.

CASGRAIN

Hold your tongue! She entered our city to the applause of the crowds led astray. That Jew of decadent morals –

MICHAUD

She was baptized a Catholic.

CASGRAIN slaps him on the back of the head.

MICHAUD

Ouch! Only her mother was Jewish. (*another slap*) Ouch!

CASGRAIN

She will be performing a play that sings the praises of adulterous love. *Adrienne Lecouvreur*, a vile play that ridicules a man of the cloth portrayed as a plotting habitué of Parisian salons.

MICHAUD

The priest is the play's comic relief! (*another slap*) Ouch!

CASGRAIN

Theatre amuses and seduces audiences, but what would be left if theatre were stripped of its dazzling ornaments?

MICHAUD

(*sarcastically*) Does the gold girdle come before or after the silver stole?

CASGRAIN gives him another slap on the back of his head.

MICHAUD

Ouch! Telling her not to perform is like telling winter there can be no snow. It's like telling a bird to clip its wings.

CASGRAIN hands MICHAUD the letter.

TALBOT

(*to MICHAUD*) How are you going to tell her, I admire you and, at the same time, I forbid you to perform? How are you going to look her in the eye and say that? What will you do when she explodes in anger? When she tells you to get out of her sight, forever? That's what your audience is wondering now.

MICHAUD

I want to diiiiiiie!

Sound of chapel bells. CASGRAIN hands a cassock and surplice to TALBOT.

CASGRAIN

Talbot, go get ready for the mass!

TALBOT

Yes, Brother.

TALBOT takes the cassock and the surplice and withdraws to change.

CASGRAIN

    (*to MICHAUD, sincerely*) I went to great lengths to convince the archbishop to choose you. (*beat*) You should thank me. (*beat*) There's no other way you could see her again. If you're not interested, I can assign the task to another student.

MICHAUD

    Never! This is my mission.

CASGRAIN

    You must limit your conversation to the archbishop's letter.

MICHAUD

    A few polite greetings ...

CASGRAIN

    The letter, not another word!

MICHAUD

    We can exchange a few words about the theatre –

CASGRAIN

    And how we disapprove of it.

MICHAUD

    A few words about my new play.

CASGRAIN

    A new play?

MICHAUD

    I've decided to write a play about poverty.

CASGRAIN

    About poverty?!

MICHAUD

    Why not?

CASGRAIN

    You were born with a silver spoon in your mouth.

MICHAUD

I've read books on the subject.

CASGRAIN

You don't know what it's like to be hungry.

MICHAUD

I'll fast.

CASGRAIN

Or cold.

MICHAUD

I'll get rid of my coat.

CASGRAIN

You should tend to your prayers instead.

MICHAUD

I'm not sure about his role, but I have an idea for the male lead in my play. There's something in his eyes. A veiled look … no, an absence. Then suddenly, without warning, a dark shadow passes.

CASGRAIN

Who are you talking about?

MICHAUD

He's a fighter. His little brother works in a factory –

CASGRAIN

(*realizing, emphatically*) You will not write about him!

MICHAUD

Why not?

CASGRAIN

Because I said so. You can familiarize him with our institution, keep an eye on him at all times, but whatever you do, don't get attached.

MICHAUD
Why?

CASGRAIN
Because I said so.

MICHAUD
Why?

CASGRAIN
He will only disappoint you.

MICHAUD
Talbot!

TALBOT
(*returning, wearing his cassock and surplice*) What?

MICHAUD
After mass, you'll come with me.

TALBOT
Where?

MICHAUD
To meet Sarah Bernhardt.

CASGRAIN
What are you doing?

MICHAUD
Wasn't I supposed to keep an eye on him at all times? That means we have to stay together.

CASGRAIN
No.

TALBOT
I want to go.

CASGRAIN
Why?

TALBOT
Curiosity.

Beat.

CASGRAIN
Very well. If that's what you want. Both of you will go to meet La Bernhardt.

MICHAUD
(*to TALBOT*) Oh, I forgot. I'm not supposed to get attached to you.

TALBOT
That's fine with me!

CASGRAIN
(*to MICHAUD*) Go get ready for the mass now. I have to speak to Mr. Talbot.

MICHAUD
What? A secret and I have to exit?

CASGRAIN
GO GET READY!!!

MICHAUD takes the other cassock and withdraws.

TALBOT
The Seminary, a cabinet minister's son, the archbishop's mass, and now Sarah Bernhardt! My deepest gratitude, Brother.

CASGRAIN
Should you need anything else, simply ask. (*beat*) I've heard about your little brother's sacrifices to enable you to become a man of God. The soul-destroying work, the terrible conditions. Fourteen hours a day, six days a week. He belongs in school. (*beat*) We're thinking of covering the cost of your studies until you're ordained. (*silence*) Do you realize how important your testimony to the police will be? (*silence*) If your tale, as you told it to the Brother Superior, is made

public, it will encourage others to speak out. It could trigger the kind of denunciations that lead to collective hysteria. La Bernhardt has attracted so many foreign journalists, I hate to think of the damage it could do if they got their hands on your story. We control the press here, but not the press from elsewhere. (*adamantly*) You must change your version of the facts.

TALBOT

God asks us to tell the truth.

CASGRAIN

God works to build his house, not to tear it down.

TALBOT

I should prepare for mass now.

CASGRAIN

Last night he was transferred here. (*beat*) He's in the infirmary. The next floor down. Do you know that he will never walk again? As soon as he regained consciousness, he told us that he forgives you. (*beat*) Your school has complained about the theft of some silverware that coincides with your departure. Whether it was you or not, you will confess to this theft. I am going to your victim's bedside. I intend to convince him to say that he caught you stealing the silverware and a fight broke out. I know he'll listen to me. I studied under him. He's an honourable man.

TALBOT

Honourable?

CASGRAIN

I would state that publicly if called upon to do so. The incident will be dismissed. We will accept your apology and you will receive a minor punishment. It's your duty –

Seminary bells ring.

TALBOT

(*showing his hands*) Look at the lines on my hands. Can you read them? It's with these hands that I will bless, that I will pardon and condemn. Look at my hands. The truth lies in them.

CASGRAIN

It's your duty –

TALBOT

I'm going to be late for mass.

CASGRAIN

On the shores of the St. Lawrence, not far from Quebec City, there are new parishes that will need young curates. There's a beautiful future for you and your family there.

TALBOT

(*looking CASGRAIN in the eye*) I'd like to have an orange.

CASGRAIN

An orange?

TALBOT

Yes! I heard that they've arrived from the south. A big, beautiful Florida orange.

Sound of bells.

CASGRAIN

It is your duty to forget.

CASGRAIN exits. MICHAUD enters and takes his notebook out from under his mattress.

MICHAUD

(*rehearsing*) "Madame Bernhardt. You? Me?" No. (*trying again*) "Madame Bernhardt. I am your greatest admirer. I know everything about you."

THE CIGAR

*The women factory workers enter and turn the dormitory
into a workshop. The beds become tables with sewing
machines and piles of shoes.*

*MRS. TALBOT and the other women, EMMA Francoeur
and THÉRÈSE Desnoyers, are lined up at the machines,
stitching red leather for women's boots. LEO is gluing
leather soles. Through the windows, spinning machinery
and conveyor belts and the silhouettes of dozens of women
factory workers can be seen. The noise is deafening. The
women work to the rhythm of the Ave Maria recited
mechanically in Latin, at rapid-fire speed. Their conversation
is woven in and out of this litany.*

EMMA
   We're runnin' out of thread.

LEO
   More thread!

THÉRÈSE
   Take one of my spools.

MRS. TALBOT
   Gotta grease my pedals.

LEO
    We're runnin' out of oil.

THÉRÈSE
    Take mine.

MRS. TALBOT
    What?

LEO
    Take hers.

THÉRÈSE
    We need black thread.

EMMA
    Which one?

THÉRÈSE
    366. Medium.

EMMA
    What?

LEO
    366. Medium.

EMMA
    Don't have any.

MRS. TALBOT
    Me neither.

LEO
    There's no more 366.

THÉRÈSE
    102 will do the trick.

LEO
    Don't see none of that either. Ma?

MRS. TALBOT
Don't have any.

THÉRÈSE
They say she's a real beauty.

EMMA
Who's a beauty?

THÉRÈSE
La Bernhardt.

MRS. TALBOT
Too many feathers.

THÉRÈSE
What?

MRS. TALBOT
Too many furs.

THÉRÈSE
What?

MRS. TALBOT
Too much jewellery.

ALL TOGETHER
What?

THÉRÈSE
They say she looks real young for her age.

MRS. TALBOT
Cow fat.

EMMA
What?

MRS. TALBOT
She puts lard on her face.

EMMA
    She puts what?

LEO
    Lard.

EMMA
    On her face?

THÉRÈSE
    How do you know that?

MRS. TALBOT
    Was in the papers.

LEO
    I'm gonna find some 366 for you.

EMMA
    That's a good boy, Leo.

        LEO exits.

THÉRÈSE
    Is she married?

MRS. TALBOT
    That kinda woman don't get married. They sleep around, that's all.

EMMA
    Well, well, widow Talbot talkin' 'bout men.

MRS. TALBOT
    What?

EMMA
    You jealous of her?

MRS. TALBOT
    Can you tell me what kinda man would want a wife who kisses
    other men in public?

EMMA

Especially with "cow fat" on her face!

> *The women laugh. Sound of the whistle as it blows to indicate a break. The women stop their recitation of the Ave Maria and the machines fall silent.*

MRS. TALBOT

For a woman who lost her two nieces last week, you're actin' pretty cheery, Mrs. Francoeur. If I was you, I'd show more grievin'.

EMMA

What?

MRS. TALBOT

I hear they seen you at a Knights of Labor meeting.

EMMA

(*proud*) That's right, Mrs. Talbot. I been goin' every day since the accident. Every day.

MRS. TALBOT

Good for you. I can't afford to get myself fired. I got a son at the Grand Seminary.

EMMA

We all know your boy's at the Grand Seminary. Nobody knows how he managed to get in, or how you're gonna pay for it, but we all know you wouldn't mind seein' your four little ones slavin' here too.

MRS. TALBOT

How dare you!

EMMA

(*furious*) You want to talk about grievin', Mrs. Talbot? I'm the one who took my nieces' bodies back to my brother and his wife. One of those bodies was missin' its head, 'cause they never found her head. You ever seen that, a little girl with a rag in place of her head? (*beat*) You ever think that her head is still somewhere in this machinery? You want to talk about grievin'? (*beat*) I know there's no gettin' rid of poverty, but I hate seein' it feed off the flesh of children.

MRS. TALBOT

You should've bought kerchiefs for yer nieces, the machine
wouldn't have caught 'em by their hair.

THÉRÈSE

For Chrissakes!

MRS. TALBOT

No cursin' around here, Mrs. Desnoyers.

THÉRÈSE

(*to MRS. TALBOT*) After everything she's done for you?!

EMMA

(*to THÉRÈSE*) You stay outta this.

THÉRÈSE

All the money she lent you for your boy's studies? You should
be grateful.

MRS. TALBOT

You don't hafta dance with your moneylender, no matter how
much you owe.

> *THE BOSS enters, dressed in a tuxedo whose sleeves are too
> long and whose pant cuffs are rolled up.*

THÉRÈSE

(*warning everyone*) Here comes the boss!

THE BOSS

(*holding out his arms like a scarecrow*) The best tailor in town!
"Tuxedo, a wool and cotton blend, with satin lapels"! He must've
mixed up my measurements with the giant in the Barnum &
Bailey Circus. Jesus Murphy! There's enough fabric to dress my
whole family. My wife decided I needed a brand new suit to go
see Our Lady of the Stage. Don't ask me why we should bother to
get all decked out to sit in a theatre that's dark as the devil's den!
(*lighting his cigar*) Don't just stand there. Fix this for me!

> *LEO enters carrying two huge spools of thread.*

LEO

I found some 366.

MRS. TALBOT

We only got coarse thread, Boss.

> *MRS. TALBOT and THÉRÈSE get needles and thread and start to shorten his sleeves.*

LEO

There was these two farmers havin' an argument in a field. The first one says, the birds are so scared of my scarecrow, they take off miles away. The other one says, the birds are so scared of mine, they bring back the seeds they stole last year.

> *Everyone laughs.*

LEO

But you take the cake. No crow in town would get near you.

MRS. TALBOT

Leo! Apologize!

THE BOSS

(*laughing*) That's okay, he's right. I look like the bogeyman. It's my wife who's dragging me to the theatre. Us men have no head for that stuff.

THÉRÈSE

For what stuff?

THE BOSS

Boredom! (*lighting a cigar*) Women love listening to people talk. Women love to talk. They yak and yak. Words, sentences, they can't stop talking. One little sentence after another, then another and another. And just when you think they've finished, they start over again. If only they had something interesting to say. But no. One sentence after another. They talk, they contradict each other, they repeat themselves. Non-stop.

LEO

Didn't you promise me a puff on your cigar, Boss?

MRS. TALBOT

Leo!

THE BOSS

A promise is a promise.

He hands his cigar to LEO.

LEO

(*taking a puff without choking*) Gratitude, Boss.

THE BOSS

Gratitude?

LEO

Dontcha know what that means?

MRS. TALBOT

Leo!

LEO

It means, thanks.

THÉRÈSE

Look at that little boss!

THE BOSS

(*to LEO*) What would you do with this shop if you were me?

LEO

I'd begin by payin' us five cents more per pair of boots. I'd cut five hours off the work week, I'd set up some decent toilets. (*beat*) And I'd put grating over the conveyor belts so nobody ever gets caught again.

The women freeze. Time stands still. Everyone fears THE BOSS's reaction.

THE BOSS
Well, if I were you, I'd start by setting up a stitching room with
a skiving machine to cut out the leather for the tops of the
shoes and the soles. That machine could replace forty cutters.
Then I'd buy a heavy rolling machine that would replace twenty
hammerers. And then I'd build an assembly room where other
machines would take care of the heels and the eyelets for the laces.
A dozen workers could run the whole damn operation. A dozen
instead of two hundred. And not a single goddamn machine
would go out on strike and parade down the streets with placards.

LEO
But there's no machine that can throw rocks at the boss,
or overturn his carriage and set his house on fire like a hundred
angry seamstresses on strike.

Heavy silence.

MRS. TALBOT
Give that cigar back to him!

THE BOSS
(*taking back his cigar*) Who taught you to talk like that?

LEO
Nobody.

THE BOSS
Was it your mother?

LEO
She's got nothin' to do with it.

THE BOSS
It wasn't your mother?

EMMA
No, it wasn't her. (*beat*) It was me.

MRS. TALBOT
Who gave you the right to put those ideas in my boy's head?!

THE BOSS

(*to EMMA*) Get your ass over here and help them fix this!

He points to his pant legs. EMMA takes some thread and kneels down to adjust the cuffs.

THE BOSS

I had a beautiful pair of boots delivered to La Bernhardt. I hope she likes them. Her visit is great publicity for our town. The whole world is watching. It should be great for business.

He puts his foot down on Emma's hand. She doesn't say a thing, despite the pain. The two other women act as if they hadn't noticed.

THE BOSS

Beautiful boots with twenty eyelets and fancy silk laces. Calfskin. A heel of solid oak. It would be a real pity if some troublemakers spoiled her visit.

LEO

You're hurtin' her!

MRS. TALBOT

(*under her breath*) For the love of God, shut up!

THE BOSS

The sleeves are fine. I'll have to find someone more competent for the cuffs.

He takes his foot off Emma's hand and exits. Silence.

LEO

(*to EMMA*) You all right?

EMMA

It's okay. I'm fine.

MRS. TALBOT takes some silverware out of her bag.

MRS. TALBOT
(*to EMMA*) A ladle, a pie server, and a carving fork. It's real silver.

LEO
You kept them?!

EMMA
Where did'ya get that?

MRS. TALBOT
You can sell them at the pawnshop on St. Paul Street. He'll give you much more than I owe you.

LEO
You shouldn't have kept them.

EMMA puts the silverware in her apron pocket.

MRS. TALBOT
Now consider my debt paid and stay away from my boy.

THÉRÈSE
Let's go take care of your hand.

EMMA and THÉRÈSE exit.

MRS. TALBOT
(*to LEO*) And I don't wanna catch you talkin' to her again.

LEO
We should've taken that stuff back to the school.

MRS. TALBOT
Have somethin' to eat.

LEO
Not hungry.

MRS. TALBOT counts the remaining pieces of silverware. TALBOT enters. They stare at each other. She closes the bag with the rest of the silverware.

LEO

What are you doing here?

MRS. TALBOT

You run away from the seminary?!

LEO

This is no place for cassocks.

TALBOT

Michaud and I are goin' to read a letter to Sarah Bernhardt!

MRS. TALBOT

Well, you ain't gonna find her here.

LEO

(*sarcastically*) You come to take your present back?

TALBOT

A letter that forbids her to perform in Quebec City.

MRS. TALBOT

I don' know her personally, but I don' think she's
gonna be pleased.

LEO

I asked you a question.

TALBOT

(*ignoring LEO*) We can't see her right away. Her manager told us
to come in an hour.

LEO

Ma, are you gonna give him what's left of the silverware?

TALBOT

I served mass for the archbishop.

MRS. TALBOT

For the archbishop!

TALBOT

It was long and boring.

LEO

What a pair the two of you make!

LEO exits angrily.

TALBOT

I want to talk to you about something, Ma.

MICHAUD enters, holding his notebook.

MICHAUD

All this leather. These spools of thread! The smell! So this is where shoes come from. I'll have to learn a new vocabulary to describe it all. My audience has to understand what poverty is like. And I have to feel what it's like before I can write about it. I always thought workers were dirty because they work too hard and don't have time to wash. My mother always told me it was because workers were never taught basic personal hygiene. Now I understand that it's not the workers, it's work that's dirty.

MRS. TALBOT

How is she?

MICHAUD

(*losing his train of thought*) Who?

MRS. TALBOT

Your mother?

MICHAUD

My parents are in London.

MRS. TALBOT

And your brothers and sisters?

MICHAUD

I'm talking too much. I should concentrate on *feeling* the environment.

TALBOT

(*to himself, exasperated*) Jesus!

MRS. TALBOT
Would you like a cuppa tea?

MICHAUD
Tea! How marvellous. Here I am in the midst of poverty and the sense of sharing remains intact.

MRS. TALBOT
You want some or not?

MICHAUD
Oh yes.

> MRS. TALBOT takes out two glass jars.

MICHAUD
We're going to drink out of glass jars! Wow! Nobody at the seminary will believe me.

MRS. TALBOT
We used to have real china cups, but real china cups get broken, and when they get broken, you hafta replace them, and ...

> She takes a clean cloth out of her apron, wipes the jars, and pours the tea.

MICHAUD
You're not going to spit in them?

MRS. TALBOT
Why'd I do that?

MICHAUD
To clean them. (*noticing her surprise*) Isn't that what poor people do? They spit in them? At least that's what I read in Mark Twain and Charles Dickens. They're writers.

MRS. TALBOT
A pity poor people don't know how to read. They could defend themselves.

MICHAUD
(*sipping his tea*) It's cold.

MRS. TALBOT

Only people who got nothin' to do get to drink their tea hot.

Beat.

MICHAUD

Downstairs I heard the workers praying. Do you always pray while you work?

MRS. TALBOT

The prayers keep the group together, help us keep the pace. Some of the women think it brings them closer to God.

MICHAUD

(*not sure what to say*) Amen. Amen, Mrs. Talbot.

They drink their tea.

MICHAUD

(*starting to rehearse*) "Madame Bernhardt. You? Me? Together?" No. (*trying again*) "Madame Bernhardt. I am your greatest admirer. I know everything about you." (*looking at his pocket watch*) This waiting is unending.

TALBOT

(*to his mother*) They're thinkin' about assigning me to a parish on the shores of the St. Lawrence. Sounds like I could move the whole family there.

MRS. TALBOT

I'm so happy to hear that, son.

MICHAUD

You'll have to teach me the names of all the tools you use.

TALBOT

I thought I could set up a little business too.

MRS. TALBOT

Priests don't go into business.

MICHAUD
That's true.

TALBOT
Maybe we could set up a little cobbler's shop?

MRS. TALBOT
I don't follow you, son.

MICHAUD
Me neither.

TALBOT
Michaud, why don't you shut up and concentrate on feeling.
(*back to his mother*) If not a cobbler's shop ... something else.

MRS. TALBOT
For the love of God, stop doubtin'. You got three meals a day,
clean clothes, a warm bed. What more do you want? Back
in that other school, one day you love your teacher, the next
day you don't. First you want to stay there 'til your dyin' day,
then you're beggin' them to let you leave. I know it's a big
deal, takin' your vows, but pray, for God's sake. There must be
a prayer to cure your doubts.

TALBOT
Ma, I think I'm not meant –

MRS. TALBOT slaps him.

MICHAUD
(*shocked*) Oh!

MRS. TALBOT
If prayin' to the Good Lord don't work, come back to see me.
(*raising her hand to slap TALBOT again*) I got more where that
came from. (*noisily gathering up the tea things*) The break's almost
over. The two of you hafta get outta here. Go see your actress.

*She exits. TALBOT doesn't budge. MICHAUD places his hand
on his shoulder. TALBOT pulls away sharply.*

49

MICHAUD
Victor Hugo says that social oppression can lead to the worst misdeeds. Your mother is clearly a victim of oppression. I'm sure she didn't mean what she just did. In fact, I believe it wasn't really directed at you. Of course, you're the one who bore the brunt, but ... it's undoubtedly due to a series of factors I'll have to examine. She can't come up with a good argument and pow! I don't think it was nice, but it certainly was spectacular.

TALBOT
Could you shut up?

MICHAUD
Should we go find some ice?

Sound of the back-to-work whistle.

TALBOT
Let's go!

MICHAUD and TALBOT exit.

A PLAY FOR SARAH

*The dormitory becomes a theatre dressing room. SARAH
Bernhardt appears in a spotlight. MEYER, her manager,
and MADELEINE, a young actress, are helping her choose
the boots she will wear.*

MEYER
The precious boots by Worth of London?

SARAH
No.

MEYER
The sumptuous Lady Duff-Gordon boots?

SARAH
No. (*waving a manuscript*) My character doesn't appear until
Act 3! The audience came for me, they came to see ME. And
here I am entering like a notary in the middle of the play, like
a soubrette who's lost her way in the story. What was I doing
for the first half of the performance? Pining away in the dressing
room? Redoing my makeup to the point of embalmment? The
author says: "Like Tartuffe, this character is the subject of every
conversation from the beginning of the play." If actors are brilliant
in the role of Tartuffe, it's because they're riding the frustration of
waiting so long in the wings.

MADELEINE
The François Pinet pumps?

MEYER
Not right.

SARAH
Meyer?

MEYER
Yes, my dear?

SARAH
Send a cable to Paris. Tell them I won't be performing in this play.

MEYER
As you wish.

SARAH
Bears! Mountains of bears! Everywhere! All around the station, masses of fur calling out my name! I've never seen so many beards, so many pelts and furs. Mama bears! Papa bears! The mayor-bear's lady-bear wife holding a bouquet of rare flowers.

MADELEINE
What kind of flowers?

SARAH
I don't know, but any flower that can survive this Siberian cold deserves to be called rare. Can you understand them when they talk? Their sentences are strung together with strange conjunctions and their verbs are missing their pronouns. They garble the consonants and swallow the vowels.

MADELEINE
You must admit that they're touching.

SARAH
Yes, when you manage to detect a toothless smile in the midst of their hairiness. How many nights are we performing in this godforsaken tundra?

MEYER
Three.

SARAH
Not easy to remake the world in three days. God had seven.
(*reciting her lines*) "Life! All my efforts, all my prayers, in vain!
Don't leave me. Soon my eyes will no longer see you, my hand
will no longer hold yours tight. Speak to me!"

   Beat.

MADELEINE
There are two "Speak to me's."

SARAH
I was taking a breath before the second one.

MADELEINE
In Boston, you took such a long breath, the curtain came down.

SARAH
That's because the second "Speak to me" was drowned in the
applause for the first.

MADELEINE
I'm going to get a breath of fresh air.

   MADELEINE exits.

SARAH
What's wrong with her?

MEYER
The troupe is tired, Sarah.

SARAH
Still no replacement for Sansas?

MEYER
No, and he's still running a fever of 39 degrees.

SARAH
Ask Belfort.

MEYER

Belfort hates that role. Who wants to play a grotesque, libidinous priest, wallowing in his fat, an embarrassment to Christianity?

SARAH

Audiences love him!

MEYER

(*handing her a shoebox*) I thought we might audition some local actors.

SARAH

Oh yes, some locals. That should be amusing! (*admiring the pair of red dress boots in the box*) They're magnificent. Look at this colour. Such an unusual red!

MEYER

A rich shoe manufacturer wanted to pay his respects. You should write him a thank-you note. The mayor has planned a tour of the city's fortifications.

SARAH

(*morose, with a sigh*) Why do they insist upon showing me the old stones of every town we visit? I hate standing in those cold places while they explain some obscure historical fact or praise the restoration of a wing I wish they had left to crumble. (*lying down*) I'm tired, Meyer! Tired of dragging my repertory from city to city, like a magician dragging his tricks from fair to fair.

SARAH / MEYER

(*MEYER says the same lines under his breath*) Tired of saying the same lines in the same tone of voice. Tired of turning my art into a routine. Or worse, a commodity.

MEYER

(*falsely reassuring*) You're exaggerating.

SARAH

I've reached the point where I hope changing my characters' boots will revive my interest in who they are.

MEYER
What's wrong?

SARAH
There are no authors writing for me anymore.

MEYER
The entire Académie is at your beck and call.

SARAH
Yes, so I can appear in the third act?

MEYER
Of course not.

SARAH
For the publicity I bring them?

MEYER
You're exaggerating.

SARAH
I don't feel wanted anymore.

MEYER
Your shows are sold out before people even know what you'll
be performing.

SARAH
Yes, the way they were in Toronto, and half the audience leaves
at intermission, once they've seen the Bernhardt phenomenon.
I'm talking about real desire.

MEYER
Of course.

SARAH
I want to be the herald of new ideas. I want to be the voice
of necessity.

MEYER
Of course, but for the time being –

SARAH

Theatre is evolving, and I am marking time.

MEYER

... for the time being.

SARAH

I need a challenge!

MEYER

(*handing her a notecard*) Write the shoe manufacturer a note.
As for the rest, we'll see.

MEYER exits.

SARAH

What's his name? (*looking for a card or an address on the box*)
Mr. Shoe Manufacturer? Dear Mr. Shoe Manufacturer! (*making
a face*) Doesn't anyone have a name around here? Mr. Mayor!
Mr. Minister! I haven't met a soul in this town who has a name.

*MICHAUD and TALBOT emerge from the shadows. Both are
wearing cassocks.*

MICHAUD

Michaud, Madame. My name is Michaud, and I'm trembling. You.
And me. Here together?

SARAH

Come closer, Mr. Michaud.

MICHAUD

She said my name! (*to TALBOT*) Did you hear that? (*to SARAH*)
I am your greatest admirer. I know everything about you. I know
that you sleep in a pear-and-rosewood coffin, padded with white
satin, lined with love letters and wilted bouquets. You had them
take a photograph of you lying in it so the whole world would
think you had died. Just to know if you were really loved. You
are extraordinary!

SARAH

I know. We know.

MICHAUD

I also know that you intend to have a tiger's tail grafted
to your body.

SARAH

That tail would have allowed me to lift my skirts behind me
when I climbed a flight of stairs, but the graft proved to be more
complicated than I thought.

MICHAUD

You are so ... so multiple.

SARAH

One day my confessor asked me to empty my mind and withdraw
into myself. "Impossible!" I told him. "There's no more room."

MICHAUD

(*laughing at her joke*) You are imperious, tempestuous.
You are a liar –

SARAH

What extensive research!

MICHAUD

You are the woman who dares say everything that should be
left unsaid.

SARAH

If you have come to replace the priest in the play, I have to be
frank. No one will believe that you or the nameless shadow
accompanying you could play the role of a priest. You are
too handsome.

MICHAUD

I don't know, Madame.

SARAH

"He doesn't know." They are the cruellest of all. And those who
know are the stupidest.

MICHAUD

We are not actors.

SARAH

Tell me another one.

MICHAUD

We are going to be priests.

SARAH

Of course, with enough rehearsal. But do you really have the
talent? I see so many young people like you who yearn to enter
this world of illusion but they are only drawn by its aura. Do you
really have the faith?

TALBOT

(*insistently*) We're not actors, ma'am. We're seminarians.

SARAH

Two seminarians in a theatre? Without catching fire? And how
many young women are lamenting their loss?

MICHAUD

I don't know.

SARAH

He doesn't know. How cruel!

TALBOT

Onstage, the character who just dropped dead right in front of us
stands up to take a bow and gets wild applause. It's ridiculous.

SARAH

Three days after his death, Christ resurrected received
a standing ovation!

TALBOT

You shouldn't joke about our Saviour.

SARAH
Now I smell fire and brimstone.

TALBOT
(*to MICHAUD*) Do what you came to do and let's go.

MICHAUD
Now?

TALBOT
Go ahead!

MICHAUD takes out the archbishop's letter.

MICHAUD
(*suddenly solemn*) We bring a message from His Excellency, the archbishop.

SARAH
(*sarcastically*) Don't tell me he'll be unable to attend my performance!

TALBOT
Read the letter!

MICHAUD
(*reading nervously*) "Madame Bernhardt. Quick to exploit man's taste for worldly pleasures, the devil presents them in their most seductive shapes. Malicious and sly, he assembles on the stage the most –"

SARAH
(*cutting him off*) Find the deepest notes in your voice, the notes that vibrate, that produce anxiety.

MICHAUD
What?

SARAH
Start over again.

MICHAUD

  I...

SARAH

You are totally lacking in authority! Start from the beginning. (*taking the letter away from MICHAUD*) "Quick to exploit man's taste for worldly pleasures, the devil presents them ..." Pause after "the devil" so we have time to imagine this demon. Look straight ahead. Frown. "Quick to exploit man's taste for worldly pleasures, the devil ..." Pause!

MICHAUD

The devil! Pause.

SARAH

You have to make us see the devil, his red face, his goatee, his deep, dark eyes.

MICHAUD

(*repeating the line*) "Quick to exploit man's taste for worldly pleasures, the devil ..."

SARAH

Pause! Imagine your archbishop biting into the flesh of actors.

TALBOT

Can't you see that she's making fun of you?

SARAH

(*sharply*) And who are you making fun of?

TALBOT

Our archbishop forbids you to perform. So there! The deed is done.

  Beat.

MICHAUD

What should I tell him?

SARAH

Tell him that many others before him have tried to shut me up.
And they failed. Emphasize, "they failed." Now leave me alone.

TALBOT

Let's go.

MICHAUD

You go ahead.

TALBOT

What?

MICHAUD

I'll join you.

TALBOT *exits.*

SARAH

Anything else?

MICHAUD

In a play, when we know the challenge the protagonist is facing,
how do we write the critical moment when he has to make
a choice? The turning point where nothing will ever be the same?

SARAH

You are writing a play!

MICHAUD

Yes.

SARAH

Is there a role for me?

MICHAUD

For you? I never dared dream ... Are you serious? (*suddenly weak*)
I have to sit down. No, I have to lie down. (*lying down*) The
archbishop's mass. My terrible visit to the factory. You! And my
new play! It's all too much. (*standing up*) It's going to be a play
about poverty. I'm just learning about the subject.

SARAH
A social drama?

MICHAUD
A what?

SARAH
It's a new trend that for the time being only attracts the converted, who, nestled in their velvet seats, delight in seeing onstage the injustices they encounter on every street corner. That doesn't prevent them from enjoying the champagne at intermission. The social realism of Russian playwrights is very popular these days. Do you know that Chekhov doesn't like me?

MICHAUD
He says you don't want to appear natural, you want to surprise and astonish. You want the audience to see you, not the character.

SARAH
(*resuming her train of thought*) Even the English playwrights are beginning to write about the working class. (*beat*) Do you know that George Bernard Shaw doesn't like me?

MICHAUD
He says you have poisoned all the great classical roles with your range of excessive emotions and unnatural facial expressions.

SARAH
Who in heaven's name are you?!

MICHAUD
"Who am I? A nameless atom,
Weary of life in mean and paltry times,
Smoking his pipe and dreaming ideals.
Who am I? I don't know. There lies my trouble."

SARAH
(*applauding*) L'Aiglon!

MICHAUD
By Rostand! Did you enjoy that?

SARAH

I'm beginning to like you.

MICHAUD

Really? I have to lie down again. (*lying down*) No one at the
seminary will believe me.

SARAH

(*smiling*) I place great hope in this new theatre that introduces
bourgeois audiences to the reality of the lower classes. Perhaps
this more socially committed theatre is the way of the future.
At least, more than the trend they call "modern" where they
imitate the sound of thunder or the sound of a train arriving
in the station and try to impress us with a machine that opens
the gateway to the heavens and makes the rain fall! A theatre
of special effects that allows audiences to leave their shrivelled
brains in the cloakroom. "Look, she's flying on cables, but let's
pretend we don't see the cables!" They call it a new theatrical
vocabulary. I call it the bankruptcy of words! Give me a refund!

MICHAUD

(*getting up*) There will be priests in my play.

SARAH

Give me a refund!

MICHAUD

It will be very moving.

SARAH

With priests?

MICHAUD

It will be new and astonishing.

SARAH

That's what the producer will say on the poster. New and
astonishing! He'll fool everyone by announcing an extended run
before he's sold a single ticket.

MICHAUD

There will be workers too.

SARAH

Their costumes will be "attractively dirty." And the actors will take to drink to get the ruddy complexion of the working class.

MICHAUD

Can you tell me how to write the critical moment when the protagonist's destiny will be transformed?

SARAH

That critical moment will come once you have exposed the different options available to him. Whatever choice he makes, there will be consequences.

MICHAUD takes out his manuscript and hands it to SARAH.

MICHAUD

I've written a few lines.

SARAH

(*reading the lines sincerely*) "My mother is cripplin' her legs in a factory, stitchin' leather that's hard as a rock. My kid brother is inhaling poison. My family's workin' themselves to the bone so I can become a priest. The only job possible for a poor kid who wants to escape poverty. "

MICHAUD

Read this.

SARAH

"A factory is the bluish stain of acids, the grey cough that drowns all melodies, the echo of a slap, the ultimate voice of reason. I wonder if the beauty of an object lies in its power to mask the suffering that went into its fabrication." It reads like Hugo.

MICHAUD

Victor Hugo?!

SARAH
Yes.

MICHAUD
Wow! My hero is a thief.

SARAH
I like that.

MICHAUD
A brawler.

SARAH
Very physical. Excellent.

MICHAUD
And there's something more intriguing.

SARAH
Go on.

MICHAUD
Instead of being punished for his misdeeds, he is rewarded with all sorts of privileges. I believe he is hiding something, something that could do a lot of damage if revealed.

SARAH
He hesitates. He doesn't know. He is facing difficult choices.

MICHAUD
Yes! He is facing difficult choices!

SARAH
But exactly what is he hiding?

MICHAUD
I don't know.

SARAH
I'll be leaving town in three days. You have to finish your play by then.

MICHAUD

Three days?

SARAH

What role will I play?

MICHAUD

Your own.

SARAH

Sarah Bernhardt playing Sarah Bernhardt? That will make
Chekhov happy.

MICHAUD

You will play the muse.

SARAH

(*making a face*) No! Not the muse! That evanescent thing draped
in veils, so translucent it's boring! I want to play the hero.

MICHAUD

You?

SARAH

Lorenzaccio! Hamlet! L'Aiglon! My fame was built on my
interpretation of male characters!

MICHAUD

I don't know …

SARAH

You are hesitating? The worth of a play can be measured by the
audience's response, my friend. Give an excellent role to a mediocre
actor and the show will close in short order. And curiously,
a mediocre script – and there are many examples – can run for
more than a hundred performances when served by great actors.

MICHAUD

The character isn't even twenty years old.

SARAH

A bit of makeup. We'll filter the lighting. (*taking back the script*)
"A priest! Not a doctor, not a lawyer. A priest! The only job
possible for a poor kid who wants to escape poverty!"

MICHAUD

(*to Sarah's astonishment*) "A priest!" Then, a pause.

SARAH

Pardon me?

MICHAUD

We have to feel the weight of his destiny. "A priest!" Pause.
"The only job ..."

SARAH

I like you. You have quite a nerve, but I like you.

> *MEYER enters carrying some floral arrangements. Sound of the*
> *boisterous voices of JOURNALISTS gathering outside.*

JOURNALISTS

(*offstage*) Madame Bernhardt!

MEYER

I can't keep them away much longer. (*to MICHAUD*) Young man,
you can be proud of your archbishop. Now, Sarah, I have to tell
you something that will make you angry.

SARAH

Now what?!

MEYER

I'm afraid your anger will make matters worse.

SARAH

I'm listening.

MEYER

They want their money back.

SARAH

Who?

MEYER

The ticket holders.

SARAH

Impossible!

MEYER

There are dozens and dozens of them who have decided not to come. Some gave their tickets to others who have decided not to come. When people wonder what they're supposed to do with their tickets, the archbishop asks them if they would feel obligated to swallow poison simply because they bought it. The archbishop of Quebec City will succeed where the clergy in other cities failed. Given the rate of cancellations, you might be playing to an empty house.

SARAH

Never!

MEYER

For heaven's sake! Read the cards that came with the flowers: "I regret to inform you …" "Due to unforeseen circumstances …" "A sudden affliction …" Do you want to hear more? I don't want the journalists to see you with him. Hide, young man!

SARAH

Why?

MEYER

The Lioness and the Lamb! The Sinner and the Saint! I can see the headlines already. Don't even tell me how old you are, young man. Just hide!

MICHAUD hides.

SARAH

This is like Feydeau! We're in the middle of a Feydeau farce.

The JOURNALISTS force their way in one after another.

JOURNALIST

What is your response to the archbishop's prohibition?

SARAH

When we played Chicago, the bishop's virulent sermons proved
to be wonderful publicity. Meyer, my manager, wrote to him.

MEYER

"Your Excellency, I usually spend four hundred dollars on
advertising in your town, but since you did it for me, I am
enclosing two hundred dollars for the needy in your parish."

The JOURNALISTS laugh.

JOURNALIST

Would you like to make a statement?

MEYER

Be careful of what you say!

SARAH

(*alarmingly calm*) I recently met a charming young man who
recognizes my true worth. He can see that I am the one who can
speak the unspeakable here.

MEYER

Take cover!

SARAH

Tell your archbishop ...

MEYER

Everyone take cover!

SARAH

... that I will answer him onstage tomorrow night ...

JOURNALIST

During the performance?

SARAH
At the end of the play.

JOURNALIST
Tomorrow night?

SARAH
Whether the house is empty or full.

MEYER
Now leave!

JOURNALISTS
Thank you! Thank you!

The JOURNALISTS rush out.

MEYER
Do you really intend to do this?

SARAH
Yes, and the performance will be sold out.

MICHAUD emerges from his hiding place.

SARAH
(*to MICHAUD*) Young man, if you want me to leave town with your play, you have three days.

They disappear.

SANDALWOOD

The dormitory becomes the stage door at the Atelier Theatre. TALBOT appears, alone. MADELEINE observes him from behind. He turns around, she smiles. In the background, the sound of a noisy demonstration.

MADELEINE
I was almost swept away by the crowd.

TALBOT
That's the Knights of Labor.

MADELEINE
They're on the rampage.

TALBOT
They're taking advantage of the journalists who've come out for The Divine Sarah.

MADELEINE
Are you the one who's going to replace him?

TALBOT
Replace who?

MADELEINE
The priest in the play!

TALBOT
What?

MADELEINE
The priest!

TALBOT
(*indifferently*) Yeah, sure.

MADELEINE
You'll have to work hard to look ridiculous. You didn't have to wear the costume for the audition.

TALBOT
You're right, I shouldn't have worn a costume.

MADELEINE
I'm an actress. Can you tell?

TALBOT
The accent. The makeup.

MADELEINE
Do you think I smell nice?

TALBOT
Perfume is perfume.

MADELEINE
When we were in Boston, Sarah said I smelled like a swamp. It's sandalwood. Would you like to smell?

TALBOT doesn't react.

MADELEINE
Are you waiting for someone?

TALBOT
My friend.

MADELEINE
Is he auditioning too?

TALBOT
Yeah, sure.

MADELEINE
Does he know that you got the role?

TALBOT
No.

Brief silence.

MADELEINE
I don't know if you're like me, but I find competition exciting.
It makes me outdo myself. Do you think I smell like a swamp?

TALBOT
It's too cold to smell anything.

MADELEINE
Try, what do you smell?

TALBOT
(*resigned*) Sandalwood?

MADELEINE
(*laughing nervously*) Yes. Exactly. (*beat*) They say there's an
opium den somewhere in town.

TALBOT
Yeah, down near the port.

MADELEINE
Would you like to take me there?

TALBOT
To the opium den? I'm waiting for my friend.

MADELEINE
When I'm not onstage, I cease to exist. We don't perform until
tomorrow night. I still have twenty-four hours, twenty-four long
hours before I exist. Is that how you feel?

TALBOT
Yeah, like you, I don't exist.

MADELEINE
Do you know why you're in the theatre?

TALBOT does not react. Beat.

MADELEINE
You must.

TALBOT
(*really looking at her for the first time*) For the actresses?

MADELEINE
Flatterer!

TALBOT
They're the only women we can really look at. Sitting there in the dark, we can look at them and have all kinds of thoughts.

MADELEINE
You have an unusual approach to the profession. Parisian actors don't talk to me like that. All they do is ask me for gossip about The Divine Sarah. I tell them, in Mexico she had a pet alligator. She fed it champagne. It didn't survive, so she had it stuffed. (*beat*) "A world tour!" They coined the phrase for her. (*beat*) It's so cold here! It's inhuman. My feet are frozen.

Unable to resist, TALBOT crouches down and unlaces her boots.

MADELEINE
What are you doing?!

TALBOT
I'm the best foot warmer in the world.

MADELEINE
Really?

TALBOT
I could warm the feet of a legless cripple.

TALBOT massages Madeleine's feet.

MADELEINE

"Flower of a single day, so beautiful yesterday, withered today, your life as short as a promise. In vain, I search for traces of our embrace." (*beat*) Answer!

TALBOT

What?

MADELEINE

Your line!

TALBOT

(*tonelessly*) "Young lady. You must renounce your profession before you die."

MADELEINE

At least you know that line.

TALBOT

What if I told you I know them all?

MADELEINE

The nape of the neck is the most sensual feature in a man. But it's often the most deceptive. When a pretty neck turns around, all too often the face is homely. (*moving closer to him*) But you are far from a disappointment. You know, I can resist everything. Except temptation.

TALBOT

You stole that one from Oscar Wilde.

MADELEINE

You seem to know a lot of things.

TALBOT

Even things people think I don't know.

MADELEINE

Do you have a name?

TALBOT
No. And you don't either. You're going to leave. We have no names.

He kisses her roughly.

MADELEINE
Gently. Gently!

TALBOT
You smell so good.

MADELEINE
Gently!

TALBOT
Too good.

MADELEINE
You don't waste time.

TALBOT
(*unable to stop himself*) How can you taste so sweet?

MADELEINE
I imagined more resistance.

They kiss again.

TALBOT
(*placing her hand on his crotch*) Put your hand here.

MADELEINE
You're breathing so hard.

TALBOT
Keep your hand there.

MADELEINE
I can't believe how hard you're breathing. I like it.

MICHAUD enters.

MICHAUD

(*approaching them*) Hugo! She said Victor Hugo.

> *MADELEINE and TALBOT end their embrace.*

MICHAUD

She said I write like Victor Hugo! Oh! Pardon me! Good evening, Mademoiselle.

MADELEINE

(*regaining her composure*) Is it customary to wear costumes for auditions here?

TALBOT

You go ahead, Michaud. I'll be back later.

MICHAUD

We have three days to finish the play.

TALBOT

What are you talking about?

MICHAUD

Sarah wants to play your life.

TALBOT

What are you talking about?!

MICHAUD

We have no time to lose. You have to tell me everything.

TALBOT

Right now, I'm going to walk the young lady back to her hotel.

MICHAUD

We can walk her back together. I love to accompany people.

TALBOT

No.

MICHAUD

Why not?

MADELEINE
Do we have to draw you a picture?

Beat.

MICHAUD
(*grasping the situation*) You can't do that! You're going to be
a priest. You'll be punished.

TALBOT
They won't say a thing.

MICHAUD
(*reciting*) "Chastity is achieved through self-control."

MADELEINE
Actors who identify with their roles are such a bore.

MICHAUD
You're coming home with me.

MADELEINE
No, I'm the one who's going home.

MICHAUD
You can't walk her back to her hotel.

TALBOT
You're right. I'm going to take her to the opium den.

MICHAUD
Where?!

TALBOT
We're going to Mrs. Chang's.

MICHAUD
Where?

TALBOT
There's a black door. You knock three short knocks and two long.

MICHAUD
How do you know that?

TALBOT
My mother's house is just behind hers. We share the same backyard.

MADELEINE
Can you afford to pay?

TALBOT
(*surprised*) I have to pay you?

MADELEINE
Not me, you fool! The opium! The room!

TALBOT
Don't worry, I have the money.

MADELEINE
Maybe we can go gambling afterwards?

TALBOT
I have all the money we need. You should take notes, Michaud.

TALBOT kisses MADELEINE in front of MICHAUD. They exit, leaving MICHAUD alone.

PIECE BY PIECE

Back at the dormitory, later the same evening. MICHAUD is writing in his notebook.

SARAH appears, dressed as a young man, as TALBOT was dressed at the beginning of the play.

SARAH

"I breathe in the sandalwood. My gestures are slow and graceful. I kiss her soft skin. United in the haze of opium, we are one. Our loud laughter drowns the whining wind of December. Giddy in the anonymous night, she clings to me. Her kisses set my mouth on fire. We walk, we sway, we almost dance our happy way to the gambling house. I bet my money. All my money. My vivacious mistress watches me take on the sailors. I feel free. They raise the stakes. I feel free. I defy my fate. I defy God. I will never be this free again."

SARAH disappears.

MICHAUD

(*closing his notebook*) "I will never be this free again."

In the background, sound of the seminarians chanting in Latin. CASGRAIN enters off to one side, pushing a trolley full of books.

MICHAUD
Brother Casgrain?

CASGRAIN
You hear the chanting? A vigil to ward off that evil woman.

CASGRAIN starts searching under mattresses and placing any books he finds on the trolley.

CASGRAIN
The Three Musketeers by Dumas. *The Brothers Karamazov* by Dostoevsky. *The Count of Monte Cristo*, also by Dumas. Once you've been ordained, you will have to enforce the *Index Librorum Prohibitorum*. Removal of works that trouble the soul and spoil innocence. You will be forced to destroy them. Diderot, Rousseau, Voltaire, Tolstoy. The Brontë Sisters. All those who question the natural order of things. You will lock away the Darwinists and anyone who defends those false theories of evolution.

MICHAUD
You can lend me *The Brothers Karamazov*. They say it's about God and free will.

CASGRAIN
(*looking under Michaud's mattress and finding his notebook*) What do we have here?

MICHAUD
Give me my notebook.

CASGRAIN
How was your meeting with the actress?

MICHAUD
My notebook!

CASGRAIN
Answer me!

MICHAUD
She is amazing. She believes in young people, as a force for change.

CASGRAIN

How did she react to the archbishop's prohibition?

MICHAUD

She will answer him tomorrow night, onstage.

CASGRAIN

God help us.

MICHAUD

She wants to perform my play.

CASGRAIN

God help you.

MICHAUD

Please give me back my notebook ...

CASGRAIN

Where is Talbot?

MICHAUD

Who?

CASGRAIN

Where is he?

MICHAUD

He must be in the choir with the others.

CASGRAIN

No one saw him come in tonight.

MICHAUD

Really?

CASGRAIN

Why isn't he with you?

MICHAUD

Because I'm not supposed to get attached to him. You were firm about that. "Whatever you do, don't get attached." My notebook.

CASGRAIN sits down on Michaud's bed.

MICHAUD
We're not allowed to sit on the beds.

CASGRAIN
Sit down.

MICHAUD sits down beside him.

CASGRAIN
Don't lie to me. I don't deserve that.

MICHAUD
I lie to you because you know I'm lying, so there is no lie.

CASGRAIN
Where is he?

MICHAUD
You don't want to know.

CASGRAIN
You have no idea of everything I do to prevent you from being expelled. I'm constantly covering for you.

MICHAUD
Give me my notebook.

CASGRAIN
I alone have made it possible for you to remain in the seminary. If it were up to my superiors, you would have been expelled long ago.

MICHAUD
I thought they appreciated me.

CASGRAIN
I try to convince them that you have a true vocation.

MICHAUD
I love God. I've read all about him.

CASGRAIN
You prefer the tragic Medea to the Virgin Mary.

MICHAUD
From a strictly philosophical point of view, they have a lot in common. Both women sacrificed their offspring out of passion. That's even harder to accept in the case of the Virgin, who knew she would – the moment she gave birth.

CASGRAIN
I pray for you all the time.

MICHAUD
Thank you.

CASGRAIN
I put up with your whims.

MICHAUD
Thank you.

CASGRAIN
I give you permission to go out.

MICHAUD
Now give me back my notebook.

CASGRAIN
Not a day goes by without my asking God to bless you.

MICHAUD
Really?

CASGRAIN
(*taking Michaud's hands*) Because, as irritating as you can be, your presence is my only joy in life. (*releasing his hands*) I won't repeat that.

MICHAUD
(*beat*) You're trembling.

CASGRAIN
(*taking a book from the trolley*) Here is *The Brothers Karamazov*. Keep it hidden.

MICHAUD
Why do you care about me?

CASGRAIN
He was insolent like you. He was imaginative and curious.
He believed in justice. (*beat*) And he was handsome.

MICHAUD
Who was he?

CASGRAIN
Someone I knew a long time ago.

MICHAUD
Why are you telling me this now?

CASGRAIN
(*gently*) I want you to know that someone is watching over you.

> Suddenly CASGRAIN grabs MICHAUD by the
> nape of his neck.

CASGRAIN
(*calmly*) Now, once and for all, where is Talbot?!

MICHAUD
I swear –

CASGRAIN
Don't swear.

MICHAUD
I swear you don't want to know.

CASGRAIN
You are a demon of the worst order.

MICHAUD
"Demon" … Then pause. Then … (*as Casgrain's grip
intensifies*) Ouch!

CASGRAIN
Tell me!

MICHAUD

Give me my notebook!

CASGRAIN

I forbade you to write about him.

MICHAUD notices TALBOT about to enter.

MICHAUD

In my play, my protagonist enters at this very moment.

TALBOT enters, dressed in a white shirt and dark pants, holding his cassock carelessly in one hand. He is dangerously calm, still a bit under the influence of opium.

TALBOT

Let go of him!

CASGRAIN

Do you realize what time it is –

TALBOT

I said, let go of him!

CASGRAIN

(*releasing MICHAUD*) Where were you?

TALBOT

In paradise, Brother.

CASGRAIN

I don't like your smile.

TALBOT

It's bliss. And my eyes? Opium. And my smell? Sandalwood.

TALBOT takes off his shirt. He stands bare chested.

CASGRAIN

I know boys like you who use their charm to obtain privileges and favours. I know them. They feign submission to get what they want. And when that no longer works, they indulge in defamation to obtain more favours. Michaud, go join the others.

TALBOT
Stay! And take back your notebook.

CASGRAIN
Leave, Michaud.

MICHAUD
I'm staying.

MICHAUD takes his notebook away from CASGRAIN.

CASGRAIN
(*to TALBOT*) I know boys like you.

TALBOT
(*calmly, provocatively*) In the beginning, the boy meets an older
man who has the eyes of a cat. And a contagious smile. He wears
an aftershave that smells of tobacco. They become friends. The
man teaches the boy to speak like a gentleman. It's important to
speak like a gentleman if you want to become a gentleman. The
man teaches him to say "gratitude" instead of "thanks." They
travel the world through books. They climb Mount Sinai and they
meet Moses. They sleep beneath the palm trees of Jericho. Then,
like Salomé with St. John the Baptist, the man spoils the boy
with presents. One day, he introduces him to theatre. They play
characters driven by strange passions.
 "Don't close those eyes that set my soul on fire.
 Those bright eyes, so loving and tender,
 They seem to share the confusion they inspire
 And leave me such a weak contender,
 I have no choice but to surrender."
Then one evening, the man asks the boy to "express his gratitude."
The boy is twelve years old. He doesn't know how. The man is
forty. He knows how. He lies down on the boy. The boy's never
felt so small. The man whispers that it's God's will. (*beat*) One
night, another night ... five years. The boy's prayers bring no
consolation. The hymns leave a taste of aftershave in his mouth.
(*walking away from CASGRAIN*) Then, two days ago ... the breath
of communion wine near his face, slimy hands groping under his

sheets ... Two days ago, the boy struck back. He beat him with one of the iron bars from his bedstead, the bar he pried loose after those stormy nights. He beat the man, not too much, just enough to make sure they'd have to call the police or a doctor, call for someone from outside who would get the boy out of that hell.

CASGRAIN

(*concerned*) If you insist upon giving this testimony, it will be your family's downfall. None of your classmates would think of dishonouring themselves by speaking of acts that should remain unspoken. Disgrace will follow you everywhere. There is no glory in becoming a shameful victim. None. Do you realize the powers you are up against? In court, the testimony of a priest who will never walk again will be more convincing than that of a delinquent who was offered all the privileges of the Church. Mr. Talbot, we must combine our efforts to ensure that the unspeakable is not spoken. You can choose between the humiliation of denouncing a horrible experience and the belief that time can heal all wounds. The choice seems obvious to me. Tomorrow you will tell the police you stole the silverware. You will tell them you fought with the priest when he caught you in the act. Tomorrow I'll take your brother out of the factory and I'll enroll him in one of our schools. Tomorrow we will put an end to this nightmare. Find in God the power to forgive and He will grant you consolation.

> *CASGRAIN takes out two oranges hidden on his trolley and places one on each boy's bed.*

CASGRAIN

They arrived this afternoon from Florida. I'm sorry, Michaud, so sorry you had to hear all this.

> *CASGRAIN exits. In a synchronized ritual, the two young men prepare for bed; they wash and put on their nightshirts. MICHAUD and TALBOT kneel to say their prayers.*

MICHAUD

"Don't close those eyes that set my soul on fire.

Those bright eyes, so loving and tender,
They seem to share the confusion they inspire
And leave me such a weak contender,
I have no choice but to surrender."
You recited Adrienne Lecouvreur's lines.

TALBOT

An innocent young woman abused by an old prince. (*surprised*)
Are you crying?

MICHAUD

(*wiping his eyes*) No.

TALBOT

Now he's here, below me. I can hear him breathing. (*beat*) He's
the one who stole the silverware.

MICHAUD

What?

TALBOT

Piece by piece. He said it was a present for my mother. Then I had
to earn it, piece by piece.

MICHAUD

You have to tell the police everything.

TALBOT

If only you knew how nice it was out there. We're walking on
the terrace overlooking the river. She wants to go home. She has
to perform tonight. She's cold. She's worried about her voice.
I place my hands on her throat. My hands warm her lovely throat.
"Flower of a single day, so beautiful yesterday ... Receive this
kiss ..." Her name is Mathilde, Marguerite, Juliette. She has many
names. She's an actress. She has underwear, so soft when you
slip your hand ... Tonight I experienced what every man should
experience. It's done.

MICHAUD

You have to tell them everything.

TALBOT
Why do you care about me so much?

MICHAUD
Proverbs. Chapter 17. Verse 17.

TALBOT
"A friend loveth at all times, and a brother is born for adversity."
Forget me. I am not your friend.

> TALBOT gets into bed. MICHAUD stands, holding the orange.
> SARAH reappears, dressed like TALBOT.

SARAH
"Was it a free man or a slave? Did he act freely or under duress?
Was he young or old? Rich or poor? Did they beat him? Did he
have children? Did his children have enough to eat? Who is the
man who picked this orange? In fact, this fruit is not an orange.
It is an illusion of happiness. From now on, this fruit will no
longer be just an orange."

END OF ACT ONE

ACT TWO

JUST ONE PAGE

The following day. The dormitory becomes the theatre dressing room. SARAH is wearing a dressing gown. MEYER enters.

MEYER

Three hundred and four. (*exiting and then returning*) Three hundred! We'll be playing to three hundred in a theatre of seven hundred seats.

MADELEINE

(*offstage*) Two hundred and ninety-six!

MEYER

There's a dozen journalists waiting outside. Don't you want to make an outrageous declaration? Maybe we could show them the alligator?

MADELEINE enters, carrying some wigs on wooden heads.

MADELEINE

The Mexican alligator?

MEYER

Yes.

MADELEINE

The stuffed alligator?

MEYER

Why not? That would give them some great photos.

MADELEINE

That would give them the fright of their life.

MEYER

Your idea of answering the archbishop onstage didn't work.
At this rate, we'll be cancelling the performance within the hour.

MEYER exits.

SARAH

This stage fright always takes me by surprise.

MADELEINE

You have stage fright?

SARAH

Don't you?

MADELEINE

No. Not at all.

SARAH

You'll see. It comes with talent.

MADELEINE

You're in fine form today.

MEYER

(*returning*) Two hundred and eighty-three.

SARAH

(*exasperated*) Meyer! Don't come back until the theatre is empty.

MEYER exits again.

SARAH

Any idea who will be playing the priest?

MADELEINE

Don't you know?

SARAH
No one ever tells me anything.

MADELEINE
I rehearsed with him last night.

SARAH
He must ooze saintliness.

MADELEINE
(*coyly*) Not really.

SARAH
Does he have a name?

MADELEINE
I don't know.

SARAH
Even more interesting.

MADELEINE
He's from here.

SARAH
A local actor. I hope we can afford him!

MADELEINE
He's very talented.

SARAH
Of course.

MADELEINE
He has beautiful hands.

SARAH
How nice.

MADELEINE
And the nape of his neck is gorgeous.

SARAH

He can perform with his back to the audience.

MADELEINE

He's marvellous.

SARAH

Oh, "marvellous men," I've known my share of them. Love –
a glance, a trance, a passing prance.

MADELEINE

I'd like to find a name for him. Louis? Arthur? Napoleon?

SARAH

Heartbreak? Betrayal? Disappointment?

MADELEINE

You're so cynical.

SARAH

It's called lucidity, and it's like stage fright. It comes with talent.

MADELEINE

Thanks for the cheery mood.

SARAH

Meyer!

> *MEYER returns.*

MEYER

Yes, Sarah?

SARAH

We're going to the factory.

MEYER

To the what?

SARAH

I've decided to thank them in person.

MEYER
Thank who?

SARAH
The owner. The workers.

MEYER
Thank them for what?

SARAH
For the boots!

MEYER
I told you to simply write him a note.

SARAH
I want to meet them in person.

MEYER
Why? To show the working class how down-to-earth you are?
What's the point? Everyone knows how down-to-earth you are.
Don't they, Madeleine?

SARAH
(*making a grand announcement*) I am preparing a new role!
And I need to know what life is like in a factory.

MEYER
(*intrigued*) A new play?

SARAH
Yes.

MADELEINE
Is there a part for me?

MEYER
Why wasn't I informed?

SARAH
It will be a social drama.

MEYER

You want us to go bankrupt?!

SARAH

I'll play a young man from a working-class family.

MADELEINE

That will require ... a monumental effort.

MEYER

We don't have time for a visit to a factory. You have too much to do. You have to rehearse with the stand-in. You're behind in your correspondence.

SARAH

(*annoyed*) I have to do everything around here!

MEYER

You haven't autographed the programs.

SARAH

Entertain people. Create a scandal!

> *MEYER and SARAH speak at the same time so that the following lines overlap.*

MEYER

I just wanted to remind you –

SARAH

Perform! Bring down the house! –

MEYER

– of your obligations.

SARAH

– Defy archbishops!

MEYER

Yesterday you said you wanted to sign all the programs personally.

SARAH

Perhaps you'd like to add to my list of duties?

MEYER

I was against the idea at first –

SARAH

Maybe there's a costume to be mended? A prop to be repaired?
Bring me some paintbrushes, we can change the colour of the set!

MEYER

You insisted –

SARAH

What would become of the world without me?

MEYER

It was just a reminder –

SARAH

I hate to think.

MEYER

Fine! Fine! We'll go to the factory.

SARAH

(*grabbing her coat*) Show the alligator to them.

MEYER

Show who what?

SARAH

The alligator! To the journalists, for heaven's sake. I'm going to get
a breath of air.

MEYER

Just leave some for the rest of us.

> *MICHAUD enters, dressed in street clothes and carrying a
> briefcase. He appears sombre.*

MADELEINE

Look who's come back. Your devotee.

SARAH

No. He is my author.

MEYER

(*exiting*) Bankruptcy!

MADELEINE

(*to MICHAUD*) Tell your friend I'm waiting to rehearse with
him. At six o'clock. In the theatre. He can give my name to the
doorman. Madeleine. My name is Madeleine. Don't forget.

SARAH

This must be how a wallflower feels.

MEYER returns.

MEYER

Now we're down to less than two hundred.

MADELEINE

(*to MICHAUD*) Will you give him the message?

MEYER

We'll be facing a deficit. A deficit! You hear me?

SARAH

Enough of this noise! Get out!

MADELEINE and MEYER exit.

SARAH

(*to MICHAUD*) How is our play coming along?

*MICHAUD takes a sheet of paper out of his briefcase and
passes it to SARAH.*

SARAH

I'm leaving in two days and you only have one page? Why?

MICHAUD

Last night I understood why my religion describes all our
impurities in such detail. I realized it's because we are bound
to become impure.

SARAH

You look pale.

MICHAUD

I also realized why Voltaire has Candide discover that we are
born neither victims nor tormentors, but a bit of both. Last night
I understood that there is no point in believing in a better world.
I realized that my ideals will not emerge from life's struggles intact.

SARAH

You should sit down.

MICHAUD

I think the only way to remain pure is to withdraw from the world
and live a solitary life. Innocence is inevitably corrupted by the
presence of others. Last night I wondered whether I will become
cynical like everyone else.

SARAH

What happened since I saw you yesterday?

MICHAUD

Read that!

SARAH

(*reading*) "You're asking me to show more gratitude? How?
My soul is troubled."

MICHAUD

(*not really listening*) It's no good.

SARAH

It's just my first reading.

MICHAUD

We have to drop the whole thing.

SARAH

Let me work on it. (*continuing to read to herself, slowly beginning
to understand*) "I'm so young. He appears like a storm cloud
threatening a summer sky. He lies down on me, he scolds me.
He casts his shadow over me. I've never felt so small. His hands,
his lips burn my body." (*realizing what she has read*) Good Lord!

MICHAUD

(*tearing the page away from her*) Yesterday my hero was rebellious and headstrong. Today he is the victim of events that cannot be told.

SARAH

Didn't you want to write about suffering?

MICHAUD

Not suffering that is vile.

SARAH

Shouldn't theatre denounce injustice?

MICHAUD

I should become a journalist.

SARAH

Shouldn't it try to bring about change?

MICHAUD

I should become a revolutionary.

SARAH

Shouldn't we believe that theatre can right wrongs?

MICHAUD

Then I should become a judge. I don't want to be a poet anymore.

SARAH

Don't say that.

MICHAUD

(*barely containing his emotion*) It's wrong to make poetry out of a friend's unhappiness.

SARAH

You know him?!

MICHAUD

(*taking back the page and tearing it up*) I'm sorry to have bothered you with this. (*quoting* Adrienne Lecouvreur, *with great conviction*) "Farewell, glorious triumphs, divine art. My heart will beat no more with these ardent emotions. Farewell."

SARAH

(*sharply*) You're right. Farewell. And don't come back.

Beat.

MICHAUD

You don't want me to stay?

SARAH

Why would I?

MICHAUD

I thought –

SARAH

I made a mistake when I took you seriously.

MICHAUD

That's cruel.

SARAH

You claim you are a poet and you refuse to write about the
wretched aspects of human nature. You refuse to depict our
human weaknesses. I believed in your naiveté. I believed that
you could deliver a fresh view of the world. I thought you were
driven by the sincere hope for change that youth alone possesses.
I believed that your naiveté would make you intrepid and
help you avoid preconceived ideas. I believed you could write
a courageous denunciation of society's ills. I must have mistaken
simple-mindedness for naiveté. Just as you mistake lucidity for
cynicism. You can leave now!

MICHAUD

Are you angry with me?

SARAH

You fooled me with a few sincere lines about the reality
of the poor.

MICHAUD

Those lines were sincere.

SARAH

Oh really? What did you see in that factory? Poverty or your own discomfort? Did you try to become one of those workers? Did you really enter the harsh reality of their daily lives? For a moment, I believed in the distress of your character ... your friend.

MICHAUD

He suffers more than you realize.

SARAH

Now I see that when the cruel reality of life reaches depths you never suspected, it makes you uncomfortable.

MICHAUD

How can I help that?

SARAH

When it comes with wounded flesh and stifled cries, suddenly suffering isn't as entertaining as you hoped.

MICHAUD

Why make the darkness of life even darker with words?

SARAH

Then go write about light suffering. Find the soothing phrases that will mask the cruelty of fate. Pander to your audience's sensations and good taste. Go write your pretty stories.

MICHAUD

(*shattered*) That's not what I want to do.

SARAH

Perhaps you are just another jovial parish preacher.

MICHAUD

(*raising his voice*) I don't know how. I don't know how to present both sides of the story fairly. I don't know how to express the aggressor's motivations. I don't know how to explain the victim's faults. A priest abuses a child! Where is the rhetoric? Where are the choices? There are no choices! No rhetoric is possible. I DON'T KNOW HOW TO WRITE DISGUST!

SARAH
Let anger be your guide.

MICHAUD
What?

SARAH
Concentrate.

MICHAUD
On what?

SARAH
Close your eyes.

MICHAUD
Why?

SARAH
Close your eyes. What do you see?

MICHAUD closes his eyes.

MICHAUD
(*resisting this exercise*) Nothing.

SARAH
What do you hear?

MICHAUD
Nothing.

SARAH
Where are you?

MICHAUD
Here!

SARAH
For heaven's sake! Do you see an object?

MICHAUD
No.

SARAH

Light? Movement?

MICHAUD

I don't want to go any further.

SARAH

A shadow?

MICHAUD

You don't realize what you're asking me to do.

SARAH

There must be a smell, at least.

MICHAUD

(*surrendering*) Yes, camphor. The smell of camphor.

SARAH

Where does this smell lead you?

MICHAUD

To another smell.

SARAH

Go on.

MICHAUD

(*opening his eyes, fully aware of what he is saying*) The smell of tobacco.

SARAH

Where are you?

MICHAUD

In a room. A white room. There's a ray of light coming from a door ajar. It's an infirmary. He is there. He is lying in bed.

SARAH

Who is he?

MICHAUD
A man with the eyes of a cat. His face is bruised from the fight.
He beckons for me to come closer. His breathing is painful.

SARAH
Go to him.

MICHAUD
I go closer.

SARAH
What does he say to you?

>Beat.

MICHAUD
I'm sorry. I can't go any further.

SARAH
So close to your goal?

MICHAUD
I can't find the inspiration.

SARAH
I don't believe you.

MICHAUD
I don't have the necessary talent.

SARAH
Fear is the enemy of talent.

MICHAUD
You have no idea of the powers I'll be confronting.

SARAH
Out of respect for your friend, you must go on.

>*MEYER returns.*

MEYER
Sarah, I can't control the journalists anymore.

SARAH
Let them in!

MEYER
Are you sure?

SARAH
Yes. Now I have something to say to them.

MEYER
(*to MICHAUD*) Hide, young man.

SARAH
No, stay here!

MEYER exits.

SARAH
Theatre, my friend, relies upon two predispositions: the predisposition to admiration, something you already have ...

MICHAUD
And the other?

SARAH
Outrage. Something you reject. Something you have just reminded me of.

The JOURNALISTS barge in.

JOURNALIST
Do you have a statement to make, Madame Bernhardt?

JOURNALIST
Your statement!

JOURNALIST
She's going to speak.

JOURNALIST
Be quiet!

SARAH

Since I arrived here, I have met members of your elite, your prominent citizens, your politicians. And I have had the occasion to observe that ... this country is retarded.

JOURNALIST

What did she say?

SARAH

History has left you behind. You submit to the yoke of the clergy who dictate your actions, your thoughts, and your words. They are responsible for the lack of progress that characterizes the most backward countries. Don't you wonder why you have no painters, no sculptors, no writers, no real poets?! You don't dare act. You don't dare rebel. It will take decades, centuries, to repair the damage done to your curiosity. There are no real men in this country, men who dare take a stand. You are a country without men.

Heavy silence.

JOURNALIST

(*stunned*) Anything else?

JOURNALIST

How dare you say such shameful things?

SARAH

Hope for change lies with your young people.

JOURNALIST

You should be ashamed!

JOURNALIST

Are you still going to answer the archbishop at the end of the play?

MEYER

Get out! Everyone! Out!

MEYER shoos the JOURNALISTS out.

JOURNALISTS
(*offstage*) Answer that question! Madame Bernhardt! Tell us!

MICHAUD
No one has ever dared say what you just said.

SARAH
Now we will play to a full house.

MEYER exits.

MICHAUD
They're going to curse you. I will never have such courage!

SARAH
Submission becomes a habit before we realize it. Then resignation becomes a *fait accompli*. Our conscience becomes muddled and we slowly begin to die. (*calling*) Meyer! Call for the carriages!

MEYER returns.

MEYER
You still want to go to the factory?

SARAH
More than ever!

MEYER
Very well. I'll call for the carriages.

SARAH
Tell Madeleine to come help me dress.

MEYER exits.

SARAH
I have no idea what one should wear to visit a factory! Young man, you make me feel alive!

MICHAUD and SARAH exit.

SCENE TWO

THE TRAP DOOR

The dormitory has become the factory. The women are washing their hands and faces in pails of water. THE BOSS enters in his tuxedo, holding his top hat (a collapsible model) and a huge bouquet of flowers.

THE BOSS
"How are you, ladies?"

ALL THE WOMEN
(*as if reciting by heart*) "Fine, thank you, Madame Bernhardt."

THE BOSS
"How are your working conditions?"

ALL THE WOMEN
"Excellent, Madame Bernhardt."

THE BOSS
"Do you like your work?"

ALL THE WOMEN
"We're one big family. One big family!"

THE BOSS
"Are you happy working in this factory?"

ALL THE WOMEN
"So happy. So happy, Madame Bernhardt."

THE BOSS
Scrub!

EMMA
We're scrubbing!

THE BOSS
Your arms!

EMMA
We're scrubbing our arms, Boss.

THE BOSS
Your face!

MRS. TALBOT
Yes, Boss.

THE BOSS
I want you looking clean as a bride on her wedding day.
"How are you?"

ALL THE WOMEN
"Fine, thank you, Madame Bernhardt."

THE BOSS
Give it more oomph! "How are your working conditions?"

ALL THE WOMEN
"Excellent, Madame Bernhardt."

> LEO enters, looking very sombre.

THE BOSS
(to MRS. TALBOT) I said I wanted all the kids to stay hidden.
Why's your kid still here?

LEO
They just found the head. (beat) Your niece's head,
Mrs. Francoeur ...

> EMMA makes the sign of the cross, and the other
> women follow suit.

EMMA
  My God!

LEO
  … in one of the machines.

THE BOSS
  This is all I needed!

MRS. TALBOT
  (*to LEO*) Did you see it? Tell me, did you see it?

LEO
  Yes.

MRS. TALBOT
  Poor baby. Try to think of something beautiful. Something
  real beautiful.

EMMA
  (*to THE BOSS*) Can I go get it?

THE BOSS
  What?

EMMA
  Her head!

THE BOSS
  La Bernhardt's going to arrive.

EMMA
  Let me go.

THE BOSS
  Why?

EMMA
  She's my niece!

THE BOSS
  I don't want to see you walking around with it.

EMMA
What ?

THE BOSS
I don't want everyone feeling sorry for you. I don't want you
making people think it's all my fault, I don't want you puttin' your
ideas into their heads.

EMMA
Are you serious?

THE BOSS
You want to know what I think? You want to know?

EMMA
I bet I'm gonna find out, if I want to or not.

THE BOSS
I think it's a helluva coincidence that they found her head just
when La Bernhardt and her pack of journalists are about to arrive.
Who's to say you weren't keeping it for the right moment?

EMMA
It's my niece's head, for heaven's sake!

THE BOSS
You can pick it up on your way home tonight! Now ... (*resuming
the rehearsal*) "How are you, ladies?"

ALL THE WOMEN
(*unenthusiastically*) "Fine, thank you, Madame Bernhardt."

THE BOSS
(*abruptly, to LEO*) Let's hear a joke. A little joke to relax the
atmosphere. Leo!

LEO
Can't think of any.

MRS. TALBOT
(*nervous*) Tell him the one about the guy who's workin' on a big
construction job. (*beat*) You know, the guy who falls from the

first floor. (*beat*) Go ahead! (*beat*) You know, his buddies are all worried, they pick him up and give him a glass of water? The guy looks at the water and says ... Go on, tell him the punchline!

Silence.

THE BOSS
Hey, kid, do I have to remind you who I am?

LEO
(*gravely*) I know who you are.

THE BOSS
Do I have to show you where the door is?

LEO
I know where the door is.

MRS. TALBOT
Tell him the punchline, for God's sake!

THE BOSS
You know what it's like out there?

LEO
I know what it's like out there. And I know what it's like in here.

THE BOSS
Get him out of my sight!

MRS. TALBOT
(*desperate*) The guy says, "What? Only water? How high does a guy hafta fall from to get a beer?" Let him stay, Boss.

THE BOSS
Get him the hell outta here!

THÉRÈSE
(*looking toward the entrance*) Boss! We got a visitor!

THE BOSS
The actress?

THÉRÈSE

No. A priest!

THE BOSS

Goddammit! I don't need a sermon today. Hide the kid!

LEO

I'm not goin' back into that hole.

THE BOSS

Get down there!

LEO

NO!

THE BOSS

Get down there, or your mother's outta here.

LEO

(*resigned but terrified*) Just don't forget to knock.

EMMA

We won't forget you.

THÉRÈSE

We promise.

> LEO disappears down the trap door. CASGRAIN enters. They
> all cross themselves.

CASGRAIN

Good afternoon, ladies, sir. I'm Brother Casgrain from the
Grand Seminary.

THE BOSS

The Grand Seminary! Well, what an honour, but I know people
more famous than you who find the time to announce their
visit in advance.

CASGRAIN

I saw the crowd gathering outside the factory.

THE BOSS
What's the occasion of your holy apparition?

CASGRAIN
I'd like to speak to Mrs. Talbot. I was told she works on this floor.

MRS. TALBOT
Is there some problem with my boy?

CASGRAIN
Good afternoon, Mrs. Talbot.

THE BOSS
Don't you think this could have waited?

CASGRAIN
I've come for your other son, the one who works here. The one who's too young to be working here.

THE BOSS
If he's too young to be working here, he's not here.

MRS. TALBOT
He ain't here.

THE BOSS
(*cutting them off*) Look, I have a Divine coming to visit with her circus, so, with all due respect, I'd like you to do me a favour and leave my shop. Come back some other day.

CASGRAIN
I heard this "shop" was in mourning.

THÉRÈSE
Mrs. Francoeur lost two of her nieces.

THE BOSS
They stopped by to pay their aunt a little visit. (*asking her to confirm*) Mrs. Francoeur?

EMMA
(*reluctantly*) That's right. A little visit.

THE BOSS

Your archbishop blessed this factory himself. A beautiful ceremony. The girls died in a Christian place. They must be dancing with the angels now.

CASGRAIN

The Church is no longer content just to bless factories, sir. We want to know what goes on inside them. Can you imagine the bad publicity if a famous actress found out what happened here?

THE BOSS

Is that a threat?

CASGRAIN

(*aggressively, up close*) Yes. And I'll confess it. And did I enjoy threatening you? Certainly, and I'll confess that as well. (*forcefully*) Where is Leo Talbot?

THÉRÈSE

Boss! Here she comes!

MEYER enters, followed by SARAH, dressed entirely in off-white. She is followed by MICHAUD and MADELEINE holding the red boots.

MEYER

(*to SARAH*) Watch where you walk. Watch out! (*ironically*) Maybe you could have worn something paler?

The women gather to form a welcoming committee.

THE BOSS

(*applauding*) What an honour! What an honour!

THÉRÈSE

(*to SARAH*) You're so ... so beautiful.

MEYER

She knows. We know.

THÉRÈSE

(*joking*) On my way home, I'm gonna buy myself some lard.

THE BOSS

(*handing her the flowers*) Sarah Bernhardt in my humble factory!

SARAH

Somehow it's hard to associate a factory with humility.
"My humble home, my humble person," but the idea of
associating a factory and humility seems incongruous. I think
you'd have to say "my humble factory" with a touch of false
modesty. Putting ironic emphasis on "humble," or perhaps –

MEYER

(*cutting her off*) She's delighted to be here.

SARAH passes the flowers to MEYER.

CASGRAIN

(*greeting her*) Madame Bernhardt.

SARAH

I can't believe how many priests there are in this country. It must
take its toll on your economy. Father? Brother? Your Excellency?
Your Holiness? We never know what to call you.

CASGRAIN

Brother Casgrain.

SARAH

(*greeting him with mock formality*) Your humble servant, Brother.

CASGRAIN

And what is the name of this young man accompanying you?

SARAH

Mr. Michaud. He wants to become a writer.

CASGRAIN

Michaud?

MICHAUD

(*uncomfortable*) That's right.

CASGRAIN
You remind me of another young man. A young man who's
supposed to be preparing for ordainment as we speak.

MICHAUD
Say hello to him from me.

THE BOSS
Somebody bring some chairs!

MEYER
Watch your coat!

THE BOSS
Bring chairs!

MEYER
(*referring to the coat*) Careful! It's a Jacques Doucet!

THE BOSS
Bring chairs for our visitors!

ALL THE WOMEN
Chairs! Here's one. Here's another.

> *The women bring chairs and place them over the trap door.*
> *Everyone sits down. CASGRAIN gets his own chair and*
> *sits down last.*

THE BOSS
"How are you, ladies?"

ALL THE WOMEN
"Fine, thank you, Madame Bernhardt."

THE BOSS
"How are your working conditions?"

ALL THE WOMEN
"Excellent, Madame Bernhardt."

THE BOSS
"Do you like your work?"

ALL THE WOMEN

"We're one big family. One big family."

THE BOSS

"Are you happy working in this factory?"

ALL THE WOMEN

"So happy. So happy, Madame Bernhardt."

SARAH

(*ironically*) Wonderful, now people answer me before I even ask a question.

The sound of knocking from beneath the trap door.

THE BOSS

Damn hammerers. They're hammering inner soles one floor down. (*playing with his top hat, collapsing and opening it*) A crush hat. It's the latest thing. Up, down. Open, closed. Up, down. Up, down.

MICHAUD

Sarah, may I introduce you to Mrs. Talbot?

MRS. TALBOT

Me?

MICHAUD

A woman devoted to her children.

MRS. TALBOT

We do what we can.

MICHAUD

Generous, firm.

SARAH

Notice how her back is slightly hunched as if she were carrying a constant weight.

MICHAUD
Yes, the rigidity at the top of the spine, probably due to all these repeated movements.

SARAH
See how anxious she looks. (*to MRS. TALBOT*) How many hours a day do you work, Mrs. Talbot?

MRS. TALBOT
That depends.

SARAH
What do you think about as you repeat these movements thousands of times a day?

MRS. TALBOT
Umm ...

SARAH
Do you have other children at home?

MRS. TALBOT
Four of them.

SARAH
Who takes care of them while you are here?

MRS. TALBOT
They take care of themselves, Madame.

SARAH
Do you find time for yourself?

MRS. TALBOT
For myself?

SARAH
What are your fondest dreams, Mrs. Talbot?

MRS. TALBOT
Dreams? (*beat*) Would you like a cuppa tea?

SARAH

How kind of you. (*making a formal announcement*) I came here –

MADELEINE

(*to THE BOSS*) So you're the owner of this factory?

SARAH

I came here –

MADELEINE

(*holding a pair of black boots*) Can you give me a good price for these boots?

SARAH

I came here to –

MADELEINE

I like the style with the long rows of buttons.

SARAH

As I was saying …

MADELEINE

I'd take two pairs.

SARAH

(*to THE BOSS*) As I've been trying to say, I came here, just before going onstage, to thank you for these boots and now I realize I must recognize the sacrifice of all these women. Come closer, Mrs. Talbot.

> *MRS. TALBOT hands SARAH a jar of tea. SARAH is touched.*

SARAH

Oh, thank you. (*raising her jar of tea, proposing a toast*) It's you, Mrs. Talbot, it's all you ladies working in the shadows, who should be thanked for this fine work. I'll wear them onstage tonight in your honour.

MEYER

Your factory's name will appear on the marquee just after the author's name.

THE BOSS

And if I provide shoes for the whole troupe ... ?

MEYER

(*joking*) Your name will appear first.

CASGRAIN

Madame Bernhardt, perhaps you could dedicate your
performance to those who died here?

SARAH

Did you say "who died here"?

THE BOSS

Don't let him cast a shadow on your lovely visit.

CASGRAIN

Tell her who died here. We're listening. Unless you don't have the
courage to tell us.

THE BOSS

Are you insulting me in front of The Divine?

CASGRAIN

I doubt that she is offended. She probably appreciates my
audacity. It took a lot of audacity to insult my country and my
Church the way she did today!

MEYER

Do you realize who you are speaking to?!

SARAH

No, no. Go on, Brother.

CASGRAIN

(*solemnly*) Yes, and tonight she'll be playing to an empty house.

MEYER

I'm afraid you're wrong there, Brother. Her comments about the
Church got theatre lovers so excited, they've decided to buy back
their tickets. But you'll be pleased to know that God has punished
them all. The price for repurchasing was doubled.

CASGRAIN

Take note, Mr. Writer. (*referring to THE BOSS*) Madame
Bernhardt's audience is composed of this breed of people!
Individuals who make their money off poor people's labour,
then ease their conscience by attending theatricals about
social injustice.

MEYER

We should leave, Sarah.

SARAH

Go on, Brother.

CASGRAIN

I know about their confessions, the most sincere and the most
intimate, and never have I heard of a single confession that
expressed remorse for the suffering of the victims of their ruthless
exploitation. When will we see a play about the two little girls
who were decapitated here, who died because their hair was too
long and the machine too gluttonous? When?

SARAH

(*terrified*) Some children died here?

THE BOSS

Only two!

EMMA

Five over the last fourteen months.

SARAH

What in heaven's name were children doing here?

CASGRAIN

They were working as slave labour ...

THE BOSS

Don't listen to him!

EMMA

And I know one head that would have tales to tell if it could still speak.

THE BOSS

You should blame the parents who beg us to hire them!
Not the bosses.

CASGRAIN

God made children as the symbol of purity.

THE BOSS

Sure.

CASGRAIN

We have a solemn duty to protect them.

THE BOSS

Amen!

CASGRAIN

It is our duty not to hurt them through our actions or our words.

THE BOSS

Alleluia!

CASGRAIN

It is our duty to preserve their purity of mind and their
physical integrity.

THE BOSS

Come down off your holy high horse, Brother. Did you ever
ask yourself once in your pious life whose little hands collected
the molasses for your desserts? Or whose little hands wove the
Persian carpets for your rectory? Who dug the gold in Africa to
decorate your churches? Should I go on?

Sound of loud knocking from beneath the trap door.

Let the writer take notes! Man exploits man. Man exploits women.
And children. Everyone knows that, but everyone pretends it
doesn't exist.

SARAH stands up and hands the boots to THE BOSS.

SARAH

You can take back your boots, sir. This red is unbearable.

Sound of loud knocking from beneath the trap door.

THE BOSS

(*furious*) Thanks for your lovely visit!

SARAH

Michaud, I'm counting on you to report everything that's happening here.

THE BOSS

When you've managed to take all the kids out of my shop, somebody will hire them somewhere else. Go ahead, tell the story, Mr. Writer! You can take the kids out of all the factories in this town. Somebody in some other city, in some other country, won't hesitate to hire them. Then people here will be poorer than ever.

Sound of loud knocking under the trap door.

(*to MADELEINE*) You wanted me to give you a good price for those boots, Miss?

MADELEINE

Yes.

THE BOSS

When a pretty woman wants a pair of pretty boots, she doesn't think about who made them. She doesn't care if the worker had enough to eat, she doesn't care if he went to mass, and she cares even less about how old he is. No. She just wants to get her pretty boots at the lowest possible price. And she doesn't wonder how we manage to make boots for that price. What colour do you want, Miss?

MADELEINE

(*uneasy*) I'm not sure now.

THE BOSS

How many buttons?

MADELEINE
I don't know.

THE BOSS
What size do you wear?

MADELEINE
(*on the verge of tears*) I'm going to cry, sir.

THE BOSS
(*to the workers*) "How are you, ladies?"

ALL THE WOMEN
"Fine, thank you, Madame Bernhardt."

MEYER
(*overlapping*) It's almost showtime. We have to leave.

THE BOSS
"How are your working conditions?"

SARAH
"Excellent, excellent." We all know.

MEYER
Let's all agree, Sarah Bernhardt never set foot in this factory.

SARAH
What?

MEYER
(*emphatically*) Do you realize what's going on here? Try to join me in reality for a moment. You can't afford to indulge in a social revolution.

SARAH
Children are dying here and we're going to stand by with our arms crossed?!

CASGRAIN
I want to see Leo Talbot.

THE BOSS
We already told you –

CASGRAIN
Immediately!

MRS. TALBOT
Why do you want to see him?

CASGRAIN
Because we can spare him the fate of the other children.

MRS. TALBOT
You show up here outta the clear blue sky, lookin' for my boy.
I want to know why.

CASGRAIN
Because the future of the world lies with children in
school. That's why.

MRS. TALBOT
Well, in my future, there's not enough money to send two
boys to school.

CASGRAIN
We will take care of that. For both of your sons.

>   *Beat.*

MRS. TALBOT
Do I have your word?

CASGRAIN
Yes, you have my word.

MRS. TALBOT
Then you can stop lookin'. He's in the hiding place.

CASGRAIN
Where?

>   *Courageously, EMMA pushes everyone aside and moves the
>   chairs off the trap door.*

THE BOSS
Mind your own business!

EMMA stamps her foot three times.

EMMA
Leo! Come out!

No reaction. EMMA opens the trap door.

EMMA
(*horrified by what she sees*) NO!

MICHAUD walks over to the trap door.

MICHAUD
Good Lord! (*placing a handkerchief over his nose because of the smell*) No, stay there, Mrs. Talbot, stay there!

MRS. TALBOT collapses. MICHAUD goes down into the hiding place.

THREE CHOICES

In the dormitory. TALBOT, dressed in street clothes, is lying face down on the floor with his arms outstretched.

TALBOT

"I take the vow of poverty. I solemnly promise before God and all present to renounce material possessions in order to pursue my search for God."

MICHAUD enters, wearing his overcoat, looking very grave.

TALBOT

"I take the vow of chastity. I solemnly promise before God and all present to never use my position to satisfy my desires born of pride or of any other nature. I take the vow of obedience."

MICHAUD

I'm so sorry about your brother.

Silence.

TALBOT

I have permission to attend his funeral.

MICHAUD

Do you want me to help you?

TALBOT

Help me with what?

MICHAUD

With your suitcase. Do you want me to help you?

TALBOT

No.

MICHAUD

Do you want your black blazer?

TALBOT

No.

MICHAUD

Your starched shirt?

TALBOT

(*standing up*) I'll wear my cassock.

MICHAUD

You still intend to become a priest?

TALBOT

Why wouldn't I? What do you think I'm doing here if don't intend to become a priest? I suppose your character, the guy in your notebook, has doubts. "It is better to hear the rebuke of the wise, than for a man to hear the song of fools." Ecclesiastes, chapter 7, verse 5.

MICHAUD

Today I understood that everything is related. I understood that poverty only breeds poverty.

TALBOT

You understood that today. There's hope for us all.

MICHAUD

Today I thought that maybe I could do something, put an end to something. That's when I decided to act.

TALBOT

You can change the world in your head, Michaud. In your head, there's nothing but illusions. I can hardly wait to see how you're going to write about Leo's death. Will he walk down a wide staircase, making grand gestures? Will he deliver tearful lines, saying "Farewell. Farewell." Will there be applause? In your play, will Leo looove to diiiie?

MICHAUD

No. There'll be a black hole that stinks of poison. There will be blood in his mouth. We will hear the sound of his fists pounding, pounding, pounding, so they let him out of there. And above him, on the trap door, while he is dying, there will be people talking, talking about the fate of children.

TALBOT

I was counting on you to make it seem acceptable. (*through gritted teeth, pounding on the wall*) Because it's not acceptable like this. Not at all acceptable!

MICHAUD

I just went to see your priest in the infirmary. (*beat*) I went to talk to him.

TALBOT

(*grabbing him by the collar*) Can't you mind your own business?

MICHAUD

I had to do it.

TALBOT

What did he say? Tell me!

CASGRAIN enters from outside.

CASGRAIN

Talbot!

TALBOT releases MICHAUD.

131

CASGRAIN

You have a visitor.

MRS. TALBOT enters, with a bag over her shoulder and holding Leo's boots in her hands.

MICHAUD

Sit down on the bed, Mrs. Talbot. Please. Sit down.

MRS. TALBOT

(*as she remains standing*) His cousin lent him his suit again. But this time, he won't be givin' it back for a while. (*beat*) I tried to remember one of his jokes. You know, the one about God and eternity. There was this beggar who wanted to borrow a buck from God and God told him to wait ... Wait, it was funnier than that. God told him ... He kept havin' those nosebleeds and I kept tellin' him ... I told 'im that you were gonna bring us happiness and relief. Yes, relief. I kept tellin' him, we just hafta keep goin' a bit longer.

Beat. TALBOT takes Leo's boots from her and tries to warm them.

MRS. TALBOT

Last night, I heard you laughin'. Like I hadn't heard you laugh for ages. I thought I was havin' a beautiful dream, hearin' my son laugh. Then I got outta bed. I realized your laugh was comin' from the house out back. Your laugh was comin' from that China woman's hell house. Your brother was right. I never should've taken your present. You brought us bad luck.

MRS. TALBOT opens her handbag and the remaining pieces of silverware fall to the floor. She points to Brother CASGRAIN.

MRS. TALBOT

(*to TALBOT*) Tell him you stole it. Go ahead, tell him or I won't be your mother anymore.

TALBOT

(*calmly*) Yes. I stole the silverware.

MICHAUD
You know that's not true.

CASGRAIN
And the priest caught you?

TALBOT
Yes, the priest caught me.

MICHAUD
Not true!

CASGRAIN
(*to MICHAUD*) Be quiet! (*to TALBOT*) And he threatened to report the theft?

TALBOT
Yes. And we had a fight.

CASGRAIN
Will you repeat that to the police?

TALBOT
Word for word. Like I just told you.

CASGRAIN
Ad majorem Dei gloriam.

> *TALBOT begins to pick up the silverware, piece by piece.*

CASGRAIN
He'll make a fine parish priest, Mrs. Talbot.

MRS. TALBOT
You won't punish him?

CASGRAIN
We will make sure that Leo has a beautiful funeral.

MRS. TALBOT
Thank you. You're too kind. Too kind.

CASGRAIN takes the silverware from TALBOT and hands it to MRS. TALBOT. Surprised, she finally puts it back into her bag. Beat.

MRS. TALBOT

Do you know what the rich think about poverty, Mr. Michaud?

MICHAUD

No.

MRS. TALBOT

They think we do it on purpose. You can write that. They think we do it on purpose. (*to TALBOT*) Let's go. Your brothers and sisters are waitin' for you.

MRS. TALBOT exits. TALBOT places his suitcase on his bed and begins to put some clothes in it. MICHAUD opens his notebook.

MICHAUD

(*reading*) "The smell of camphor. The glow coming from a door ajar. The painful breathing of the man lying in bed punctuates the silence. My footsteps are betrayed by the creaking of my shoes on the waxed floor boards. I stare at him. Rosary beads slip through his broken fingers. Hail, Mary … He gasps for breath. Hail, Mary, full of gasps. His broken nose, his bruised cheek. He returns my look. He knows why I have come. His swollen tongue loosens." (*taking a letter from between the pages of his notebook*) Here is his confession signed in his hand. He confesses everything that he did to you. Now my hero has three choices. Either he gives this letter to the authorities and awaits the strange justice of men, the justice that condemns the criminal and stains the victim forever. (*beat*) Or he gives it to his mother so they can both find consolation in the truth and share the pain. Or he tears it up and keeps his secret forever. Now he must choose the consequences.

MICHAUD hands the letter to TALBOT.

TALBOT

(*speaking as if he were rehearsing his vows the day of his ordainment*)
My name is Joseph Talbot. I'm going to become a curate in
a beautiful parish on the shores of the St. Lawrence.

TALBOT tears up the letter without reading it and exits.

CASGRAIN

Thank the Lord. It's all over.

*MICHAUD goes to pick up the pieces of the letter and
recites it by heart.*

MICHAUD

"Your Excellency. I have attached a list with the names of
the young students who were under my direction over the
years. In an unforgivable abuse of my authority, I subjected
these students to my most selfish instincts. I humbly ask you
to exclude me from my order and to deliver my letter to the
authorities so that I am submitted to human justice."

Shaken, CASGRAIN sits down on a bed.

CASGRAIN

Was Talbot's name on the list?

MICHAUD

Yes. (*putting on his winter coat and picking up his cassock*) Tonight
I will wear this costume for the last time.

CASGRAIN

If you go to the theatre tonight, you will never set foot here
again. And no other institution will admit you. I will see to that
personally. Do you hear me? A flash in the pan. Your actress's visit
is just a flash in the pan. Now that she has opened your eyes to see
the world around you, and opened your heart to feel the suffering
of others, what are you going to do? As soon as she leaves this
city, the darkness that will descend will be deeper than ever. She
is right about what is happening here. You know now that outside
these walls, there is ignorance, vulgarity, and scheming. There

is nothing but water carriers, smoke inhalers, shit slingers, pale eyes, and cold hands. They stay hidden in dark shops and filthy factories. At the end of the day, they curse God and guzzle their cheap wine. At night, they dream of the devil and, on Sunday, they become holier than thou. Do you really think you can change that? By writing pretty sentences to convince yourself that the revolutionary army is on the march, that it will force its way into every household, waving silk banners and shouting inspiring slogans?! We cannot change the world, Michaud. There is no way. A force greater than us decides everything. Decides how we live, how we behave, how we speak. That force decides what we eat, who we choose to love, and it decides how we will die. That force is omnipresent and complex. It has no face, no name, and it is not accountable. It dictates our lives, our every decision. It reminds us of our impotence. It exploits love. It exploits our longings, our senses, our weaknesses, and our indifference to knowledge. It exploits our grudges as well as our aspirations. Reread the history of the world. Read all the forbidden books. This perpetual, inextricable force fashions our illusions and manipulates our hopes. That force is called Power and there is no point in becoming a martyr in an attempt to overthrow it. It will always exist. We will always replace one power with another, in the name of a god or a king, in the name of a chosen race or our right to comfort and the pursuit of happiness. Your theatre, Michaud, is as benign as a sermon in the celebration of the mass. (*moving uncomfortably close to MICHAUD*) You must find happiness in submission. Submit with talent. Find the advantages to serving. Use your conscience as the means to reach the highest offices. Stand at the master's side without ever contesting him. With every breath you take, remind him that you are glad to be his subject. Stay here. Stay with me!

MICHAUD

Who was it? The person you knew who had my insolence? And who was curious? (*silence*) He was imaginative. He believed in justice. (*beat*) That person was you, wasn't it? (*beat*) Your name is on his list. The first name on his list. (*beat*) He said he abused you for three years. I'm sorry.

CASGRAIN

Promise me that this will remain between the two of us.

MICHAUD

(*indicating the pieces of the letter*) The letter.

CASGRAIN

What about it?

MICHAUD

That was a copy. I took the original to the police ... along with the list of names. Outrage serves no purpose if there is no justice.

Sound of the seminary bells ringing.

CASGRAIN

(*ashen*) Time for mass. The bells are ringing for mass. Do you hear them?

SCENE FOUR

EPILOGUE

The dormitory becomes the stage and the wings of the theatre. SARAH and MADELEINE are performing Adrienne Lecouvreur.

MADELEINE

(*acting, close to SARAH*) "Flower of a single day, so beautiful yesterday, withered today, your life as short as a promise. In vain, I search for traces of our embrace! Receive this parting kiss that bids you farewell forever."

SARAH

(*playing the role of* Adrienne Lecouvreur *on her deathbed*) "Life! All my efforts, all my prayers, in vain! I feel my strength and my life slipping away. Don't leave me. Soon my eyes will no longer see you, my hand will no longer hold yours tight. Speak to me! Speak to me!"

MADELEINE

(*acting*) "She is dead, the poor child."

SARAH

(*improvising*) No. Not quite.

MADELEINE

(*improvising reluctantly*) Something else?

SARAH

Yes.

MADELEINE

She wants to say something else?

SARAH

Yes, I believe I have something else to say to someone.

MEYER

(*in the wings*) Good Lord! What are those lines?

SARAH

(*improvising*) Father, come out of the shadows!

> MICHAUD *appears onstage, wearing his cassock and holding his play in his hands.*

MEYER

(*in the wings*) Where did he come from?! What is he doing here?!

MICHAUD

(*playing the role of the priest*) "Young lady! You must renounce your profession before you die."

SARAH

(*to MICHAUD*) Face the audience, Father!

MICHAUD

(*facing the audience*) "Renounce your profession!"

MEYER

(*in the wings*) She's dead! She's dead, for God's sake! Curtain!

SARAH

(*directly to the audience, improvising*) You want me to renounce my profession as an artist?

MICHAUD

(*playing the role of the priest*) "Yes, my child."

SARAH

Do you really know the art you are cursing?

MEYER

(*in the wings*) Good heavens, she's going to answer the archbishop.

SARAH

You are asking me to abandon the theatre?

MICHAUD

(*playing the role of the priest*) "Yes, my child."

SARAH

You want me to scatter to the four winds the divine emotions it has brought me? Me? One of the high priestesses of this art? You want me to renounce it?

MICHAUD

"Renounce!"

SARAH

Theatre is the sister of History and Philosophy, of Politics and Justice. It is the love of everything good and beautiful. What would life be without art? Eating, drinking, sleeping, praying, dying? Why go on living? Theatre gently preaches what you preach so harshly. When it portrays vices, it's so we can better overcome them. Theatre reveals turpitude and excess. It denounces tyrants by portraying their tyranny. It educates the ignorant without their realizing it. It opens our minds. It touches our hearts. It punishes. It pardons. It seeks the truth.

MICHAUD

(*playing the role of the priest*) "Repent, my child."

SARAH

Through the theatre, we can become a father who sacrifices his daughter to appease the gods. We become the young lovers in Verona who love each other despite their differences. We become a man with a long nose who is pining for his beautiful cousin. We become the young man who, imprisoned in the solitude of a dormitory, imagines his unlikely meeting with a famous actress. The young man who, touched by the fate of his friend, dares to portray the harshness of his times. (*resuming the text of the play* Adrienne Lecouvreur) "Farewell, glorious triumphs, farewell, divine art. My heart will beat no more with these ardent emotions! Farewell, my dear friends … !"

Applause and bravos that slowly fade out.

Back in the dormitory. MICHAUD takes off his cassock as he speaks.

MICHAUD

She received one of the longest ovations of her career. The boisterous reaction of the students attending the performance, those who dared defy the authority of the archbishop, could be heard as the actors took their bows. Throughout the curtain calls, baskets of flowers were lowered onto the stage. Along with paper doves wearing ribbons around their neck, bearing sonnets for The Divine Sarah. But outside the theatre, hundreds of people gathered, pushing and shouting. On the one hand, dozens of bigots cursing Sarah, and on the other, the Knights of Labor insulting the people who came out of the theatre. When Sarah appeared, the furious crowd started hurling rotten eggs, chunks of ice, and cobblestones. Two members of the troupe were injured in the chaos. Sarah and her troupe left Quebec City in a panic. (*taking out his suitcase and packing his belongings*) I tried to catch up with Sarah to give her my play. I ran, waving my play. Swept away by the angry crowd, all the way to the train station. In the midst of the shouts and insults. Waving my play. I stood on the platform and watched the train disappear in the distance. Waving my play for Sarah. On her car, on her beautiful Pullman, they had painted: "Go home, dirty Jew." And I stood on the platform, waving my play.

While MICHAUD speaks, CASGRAIN enters with the ladder and places it beneath the window. He removes his shoes and, taking them in hand, climbs the ladder, opens the window, and leaves his shoes on the sill. He then climbs down the ladder and exits.

MICHAUD

Newspapers throughout North America and Europe were scandalized by this treatment of such a great artist. The prime minister of Canada offered his personal apology. (*beat*) The archbishop became a cardinal. The priest with the eyes of a cat was sent to Africa. Censorship of books and theatre performances increased. Several days later, Brother Casgrain's body was found in the courtyard of the Seminary. They said he fell from the dormitory window.

Sound of the seminarians chanting in the background. TALBOT enters, wearing a cassock and pushing the trolley full of forbidden books. He looks under a mattress, finds a book, and places it on the trolley. MICHAUD empties the contents of his suitcase onto the floor and fills it with books from the trolley.

MICHAUD

(*to TALBOT*) I finished my play. (*handing it to TALBOT*) Here! (*about to leave*) Talbot?

TALBOT

What?

Confidently, MICHAUD goes to take TALBOT in his arms.

Beat.

As the lights go down, MICHAUD picks up his suitcase and exits, leaving TALBOT, who opens the notebook and begins to read.

SARAH appears, dressed as TALBOT was dressed at the beginning of the play.

SARAH

"My gestures are slow and graceful. I kiss her soft skin. United in the haze of opium, we are one. Our loud laughter drowns the whining wind of December. Giddy in the anonymous night, she clings to me. Her kisses set my mouth on fire."

Blackout.

THE END

ACKNOWLEDGEMENTS

This play was written thanks to the generous invitation and exceptional support of the prestigious Shaw Festival at Niagara-on-the-Lake. The play was inspired by the work of the Irish playwright George Bernard Shaw, who denounced the ravages of capitalism and the hypocrisy of the religious hierarchy.

My thanks to Jackie Maxwell, for her enthusiasm and her confidence in my work. Thank you to all the actors and actresses at the Shaw Festival and at Montreal's Théâtre du Nouveau Monde who participated in the workshops and readings. Thank you to Linda Gaboriau, for her precious advice and for embracing the challenge of translating into English the numerous drafts of this play.

Thank you to Lorraine Pintal and the team at Théâtre du Nouveau Monde in Montreal for presenting *La Divine Illusion*, a premiere of the original French version of the play in November 2015.

Thanks to everyone at Talonbooks.

And finally, thank you to Louis Gravel, my favourite reader.

ABOUT THE TRANSLATOR

LINDA GABORIAU is an award-winning literary translator based in Montreal. Her translations of plays by Quebec's most prominent playwrights have been published and produced across Canada and abroad. In her work as a literary manager and dramaturge, she has directed numerous translation residencies and international exchange projects. She was the founding director of the Banff International Literary Translation Centre. Gaboriau has twice won the Governor General's Award for Translation: in 1996, for Daniel Danis's *Stone and Ashes*, and in 2010, for Wajdi Mouawad's *Forests*.

ABOUT THE AUTHOR

MICHEL MARC BOUCHARD emerged on the professional theatre scene in 1985. Since then he has written twenty-five plays and has been the recipient of numerous awards, including, in June 2012, the prestigious National Order of Quebec for his contribution to Quebec culture, and, in 2005, the Order of Canada. He has also received le Prix Littéraire du Journal de Montréal, Prix du Cercle des critiques de l'Outaouais, the Governor General's Performing Arts Award, the Dora Mavor Moore Award, and the Chalmers Award for Outstanding New Play. Translated into nine languages, Bouchard's bold, visionary works have represented Canada at major festivals around the world.